The Quilt Inn
Country
Cookbook

Aliske Webb

The Quilt Inn Printworks Inc

1993

Copyright 1993 by Aliske Webb
All rights reserved

The Quilt Inn Printworks Inc.
24 Farmcrest Drive
Scarborough, Ontario
M1T 1B7

Printed in the USA
First Quilt Inn Printworks Printing: September 1993
10 9 8 7 6 5 4 3 2

ISBN 0-9696491-2-6

ATTENTION: SCHOOLS AND CORPORATIONS

The Quilt Inn Printworks Inc. books are available at quantity discounts with bulk purchase for educational, business, or sales promotional use.
For information, please write to:
    Special Sales Department
    The Quilt Inn Printworks Inc.
    24 Farmcrest Drive
    Scarborough, Ontario
    Canada M1T 1B7

To Gail and Gerry

*Good friends, gracious hosts
and fellow travellers
who dare to follow
the path less travelled*

Introduction

The Quilt Inn Country Cookbook was written as an invitation for you to join us at The Quilt Inn, to savor not only the joy of bountiful down-home cooking, but to drink in the pleasures of country inn living. We are itinerant travellers and country inn lovers, and we have selected and savored the best recipes of all the ones that we have tried, to create the essence of "inn-ness" for you. We've collected our favorite dishes, and memories, and spread them out for you here on our harvest table for you to sample and enjoy. When you re-create these recipes for yourself, and as the homey smells of country cooking waft through your own kitchen, we hope you will be transported to the Quilt Inn where a warm welcome awaits you.

People often ask us where The Quilt Inn is located, and when can they come to visit us. The Quilt Inn is that mythic sort of place, like Camelot, that rises up unexpectedly and fortuitously at the end of a long day to give haven to the weary traveller. We've all been to The Quilt Inn, if only in our hearts. The Quilt Inn is old and cozy, just like one of Grama's beloved and faded quilts it was named for. Whenever we are weary and bleary-eyed we can wrap it around us, and sink into its comfort.

In Spring we find the Inn nestled in a cozy blanket of snowy white cherry and peach blossoms. In Summer we find it perched atop a breezy hill where the verdant treetops rustle like yards of crisp taffeta swooshing overhead. In Fall we find it at the end of a long narrow lane bordered by rows of trees in riotous colored patchwork. In Winter we find it etched sharply in delicate filigrees of ice as our footsteps crunch noisily across the snowy fields.

It is everywhere different, and everywhere the same. It is the best of welcoming places.

Welcome to The Quilt Inn.

Aliske Webb, September 1993

Table of Contents

You may find The Quilt Inn Country Cookbook to be an unusual sort of book. It's a combination of stories about country inn living, and stories about quilting, along with simple and easy recipes. Each chapter starts with a story that leads into the recipes that follow. Recipes were grouped by theme rather than normal food grouping.

Introduction

Everybody's From Somewhere   2

Swing Time   4
Cool drinks to sit an' sip

Bandits at Four O'Clock   6
Breakfast favorites

Adam's Search for the Ultimate Rib   20
Great rib recipes

Sittin' Loose   36
Picnic fare

Tomatoware - Tomatofare   46
What else -- tomato recipes

Hunka Hunka Burnin' Love   56
Hot chili stuff

Who Will Pick Up My Stitches When I'm Gone?   64
Casseroles

The Wrong Arm of the Law   70

Desserts

Send The Servants To The Cellar   78
Lowly cabbage cecipes

It's All Greek To Me   92
Favorite Greek recipes

Lionhearts   106
Hearty Stews

Loose Change   116
Sauces to add a little spice

Sunday, Sunday   124
Brunch recipes

A Lifestyle in Provence   134
South of France cooking

Midnight Stars   142
Star-gazing party fare

What's My Wine?   148
Recipes with spirit

The Orchard   158
Peach recipes from start to finish

Canned Laughter   164
Preserves and canning

Songs From The Hearth   170
Breads and rolls

Giving Thanks   178
Super soups

Holiday Memories   190
Seasonal recipes for the holidays

Everybody's From Somewhere

As Michael and I travelled around the country collecting stories for our memories and recipes for the Inn, we've enjoyed visiting small towns everywhere. I avoid highways whenever possible and go out of my way to find the "grey roads" on the map. I often get us lost, but even that's OK. Getting lost often leads you to someplace more interesting. Strange, that.

Early on we noticed that every town we visited inevitably had a sign at the town limits proudly boasting a native son or daughter who had gone on to fame and fortune, supposedly elsewhere. Now we're on the lookout for those wonderful telltale signs. I think we've found the home of every Miss America since 1957. We found football, basketball and baseball stars who made it past local high school hero to world class competitor. We found singers and musicians who probably drove the neighbors crazy, were the ne'r-do-wells at the time, probably now laughing, and strumming, all the way to the bank.

In the Who's Who of towns, (or perhaps that should be the Where's Where), is there a pecking order of luminaries? If your town boasts only a Regional Whatever Championship 19--, are you less of an address than a town boasting a Miss America, or a Hall of Famer?

It's a comfortable reminder that everybody is from somewhere. And driving around any somebody's hometown lets us see a glimpse of their past, and perhaps their motivation for acheiving success, elsewhere. We wonder how those hometowns fare in their memories -- happy nostalgia of childhood, or couldn't wait to leave nightmares.

All those towns are everywhere different and everywhere the same. They are towns without pity, towns from hell, or even towns with no name (supposedly Clint Eastwood characters live there). It may be twenty-four hours from somewhere, or 1,000 miles from nowhere. Or even south of the border.

And every town has the same sides. Every town has its uptown, downtown Saturday night. Its ever musical east side, west side. Inevitably some good old boy is headed for the cheating side of town, while someone else is coming back from heartache avenue to the lonely side of town. There's the seamy side of town, where skid row is. There are girls from the bad side of town and boys from the wrong side of the tracks having back street affairs.

That's a lotta sides for one town.

You may have got there from the mean streets, or easy street. You may have taken the straight and narrow, or the long and winding road. Or even the yellow brick road. If you're street smart, take the streetcar named desire back to the street where you live, on the sunny side of the street.

Yet wherever we journey away to there are always blue highways that lead you to the back roads by the river of your memories, ever smiling, ever gentle on your mind.

Swing Time

On warm lazy afternoons I like to take a cool drink and lie in the hammock. It's located in the middle of the front lawn, so it's far enough away from the verandah that no one can easily talk to you and disturb your reveries, yet close enough to be summoned if needed. Michael has learned that it requires a three alarm fire to warrant calling me out of the hammock. It's a place I need to go to when I'm mad at him for some reason or other. As Goethe said, "In a good marriage we become the guardians of each other's solitude."

The hammock came to live with us from Mexico. It used to be gaudy fiesta colored but it's toned down somewhat and mellowed out a lot since, and I believe it's trying to approach a respectable earth tone appearance in order to fit into our decor. It's slung between two huge century trees, centurian trees. One willow; one oak.

When the trees were originally, and symbolically, planted in the farmyard they were appealingly close together. Now that they are monster trees, they are far too close together and make an odd coupling. The bent-over willow with its long slender, supple leaves that swish softly in the wind and symbolizes flexibility and change, stands beside the starchy upright oak with its broad stiff leaves that rustle crisply and irritably, and symbolizes strength and stability. These are trees that speak two different leaf languages. Yet like yin and yang, they are opposites that complement and complete each other into a wholeness.

Their branches intertwine bizarrely. The willow seems to flow into the oak's stiff embrace, like an oddly coupled marriage. An artificially arranged marriage at that. Yet here they are, generations later, still standing side by side, rooted and symbiotic. They've grown around each other, accommodated each other. Given each other space to grow. If one were to be cut down now, there would be spaces among the remaining one's branches, like an empty embrace. Yes, just like a marriage.

And here I lie swinging between the two trees.
Sometimes I am willow; sometimes I am oak.

✳ ✳ ✳

Cool drinks to sit n' sip with. The most famous classic of all, I think...

Mint Julep

1 tsp Sugar
1 tsp Water
4 fresh Mint leaves
Fine crushed Ice
3 oz Bourbon
1 fresh Mint sprig

Combine sugar, water and ice in tall chilled glass until sugar is dissolved. Add ice to three-quarters full. Add bourbon and stir gently. Freeze for 15 minutes. Garnish with mint sprig before serving.

Summer Punch

16 2-cup Teabags
3 qt Water
1 c Sugar
1 can frozen Lemonade concentrate
1 32-oz bottle Ginger ale

Bring water to a boil and add teabags. Remove from heat, cover and let stand 10 minutes. Discard teabags. Add sugar and lemonade, stirring until sugar dissolves. Chill thoroughly. Stir in chilled ginger ale just before serving.

Bandits at Four O'Clock

One of the great things about Inn life is you get to rise early in the morning when it's peaceful, cool and dark, to prepare breakfast for the guests. Great if you're a robin, not so great if you're an owl. And four o'clock is earlier than anyone needs to get up. That's the time when the banging and clattering started in the garden shed, behind the "summer kitchen".

The summer kitchen is a later wood-frame addition to the original stone house. A summer kitchen was used, as the name implies, during the summer when it was hot, so that the cooking stoves wouldn't heat up the otherwise cool main house. It was also where the women put up preserves and processed all the garden produce for winter. I can't imagine how uncomfortable it must have been when they were cooking and canning during the hot, hot days of summer, before air conditioning or even electric fans. The original small wood door has now been enlarged into an archway that connects it directly to the big main kitchen. The shed that is attached to the summer kitchen is accessible only from the outside, but the hollow wood walls boom loudly with the echoes from the banging within.

Back in the city, night noises like this would have panicked me. But here I know that whatever is making the noise is probably more afraid of me than I am of it. Probably rightly so. Humankind has done more damage to nature than nature has ever done to us.

So, I pulled on a sweater and crept quietly to the kitchen and rummaged in the junkdrawer for a flashlight. The steps were cold and wet beneath my bare feet, but I never care about that when I'm hunting out my friends.

As I creaked open the shed door and shone the light around inside, scurried rustlings behind the wheelbarrow revealed my quarry. A litle pointy face stared back at me. Then two, three, four more culprits popped into view. Caught red-handed, four black-masked bandits were stuffing themselves with birdseed that Michael forgot to store in a metal storage bin.

Momma raccoon had returned, with three babies this year. She's never quite comfortable with humans, not like city park raccoons, and I don't want to tame her. That's too dangerous for her and her babies. She's better off wild and fearful of humans. Momma raccoon has only three legs. I often wonder what happened to her. A fight with a farmyard dog maybe, or caught in a trap, or whatever; she's a tough old survivor.

I left the shed door open and backed off a dozen feet so I could watch them. That way, they could continue foraging in comfort.

After a few minutes Mother ambled unconcerned out the door and the three kits followed in a panic. She walked off thirty feet or so and sat down, and looked back. All her babies were there behind her. She looked at me, sat up and rubbed her whiskers as if to say, "Thanks for the breakfast," and then rubbed her ear in farewell. Off they went back into the darkness.

Back in bed with ice cold feet, Michael opened his eyes, looked at me and shook his head smiling. He knows that tomorrow night the birdseed will be stored away properly and the shed door will be locked, and that I'll leave out some scraps before we go to bed. Maybe even some bacon from this morning's breakfast at the Inn.

Eggs Benedict

1 1/2 tbsp Butter
1 1/2 tbsp all-purpose Flour
1 1/4 c Milk
3/4 tsp dry Mustard
1 tbsp Lemon juice
1/4 tsp Hot sauce
1/2 c grated Parmesan cheese

Quilt Inn Country Cookbook

2 English Muffins, split
2 slices thick cut Ham, back bacon or peameal bacon
4 Eggs
2 tbsp chopped fresh Parsley

To prepare sauce: Melt butter in saucepan. Whisk in flour. Cook 2 to 3 minutes on low heat, stirring but not browning. Whisk in milk. Bring to boil. Reduce heat. Simmer for 5 minutes. Stir in mustard, tabasco, lemon juice, cheese and salt and pepper to taste.

Toast muffins. Butter lightly. Place on cookie sheet. Keep warm in oven. Warm ham in oven.

Poach eggs. To serve, place slice of ham on each muffin, top with egg. Pour on sauce. Sprinkle with parsley.

Apple French Toast with Cinnamon Sauce

4 Eggs
1 c Milk
3 tbsp Sugar
1 tsp Vanilla
1/2 tsp Cinnamon
8 slices day old French bread, cut thick
3 tbsp melted Butter

Preheat oven to 375F

French Toast is better made with day old bread. It will soak up the egg more than too-fresh bread will and it will puff up more.

To prepare toast: Whisk eggs with milk, sugar, vanilla and cinnamon. Dip bread into mixture, coating both sides, allowing bread to soak up mixture. Place bread in single layer on baking sheets brushed with butter to prevent sticking. Bake for 12 minutes; turn bread over; bake another 12 minutes or until brown and puffy.

Sauce:
2 tsp Butter
1/2 c Brown Sugar
1/3 c Water
1/2 tsp Cinnamon
3 Apples, peeled, cored and sliced thinly

To prepare sauce: Add butter and sugar in saucepan. Cook until melted. Add water, cinnamon and apples. Cook on low heat for 8 to 10 minutes, or until tender.

To serve: Arrange toast on plate, top with sauce.

Christmas Toast

The use of nutmeg in this classic French Toast recipe gives it a distinctive Eggnog flavour. It's great anytime of the year, but at Christmas, substitute Eggnog for milk.

4 Eggs
1 c Milk
3 tbsp Sugar
1 tsp Vanilla
4 tsp Nutmeg
8 slices French bread, cut thick
3 tbsp melted Butter

Preheat oven to 375F

To prepare toast: Whisk eggs with milk, sugar, vanilla and nutmeg. Dip bread into mixture, coating both sides, allowing bread to soak up mixture. Place bread in single layer on baking sheets brushed with butter to prevent sticking. Bake for 12 minutes; turn bread over; bake another 12 minutes or until brown and puffy.

Serve with icing sugar "snow" dusted over the toast, mint leaves and a dollup of red current jam to resemble Christmas holly.

Rice Pudding is one of my all time favourite breakfasts and a great way to use up left over cooked rice from last night's Chinese dinner. In fact, whenever I cook steamed rice I always make twice what I need so I know I'll be able to make "rice puddy" for breakfast.

"Leftover" Rice Pudding

2 c cooked Rice
1 c Milk
2 Eggs
1/2 c Sugar
1 tsp Cinnamon
1/2 tsp Nutmeg
1 c Raisins

Preheat oven to 350F. Blend milk, sugar and egg together. Bring to boil and stir until mixture begins to thicken. Pour over rice in casserole dish. Mix in raisins and spices. Bake 40 to 50 minutes, stirring occasionally to prevent sticking or separating.

From Scratch, Creamy Rice is Nice Pudding

1/3 c Rice
4 c Milk
2 tsp Cornstarch
1/3 c Sugar
1/2 c heavy Cream
2 Apples, peeled, cored & chopped
1/2 c raisins
2 tbsp Butter
1/4 c Brown Sugar
1 tbsp Cinnamon

Heat rice and milk in saucepan until milk comes to boil. Meanwhile, combine cornstarch and sugar. Whisk in cream until mixture is smooth. Whisk into hot milk/rice mixture. Reduce to low heat. Cover and cook 40 to 55 minutes or until rice is thick and creamy, stirring occasionally.

While rice is cooking, combine apples, raisins, butter, brown sugar and half the cinnamon in saucepan. Cook 20 to 30 minutes on low heat until apples are tender and mixture thickens.

To serve: Pour rice into large casserole or individual dishes. Top with apple mixture. Sprinkle with remaining cinnamon. Serve warm or cold.

Corn bread is a dish that goes back to pioneer days when the Indians first taught the settlers how to prepare the dried cornmeal. This recipe goes equally well with breakfast or as a dinner roll when made in individual muffin pans.

Spicy Cornbread

1 1/2 c all-purpose Flour
1 c yellow Cornmeal
2 tbsp Sugar
4 tsp Baking powder
3/4 tsp Salt
1/2 tsp Chili powder
1 1/4 c Milk
2 large Eggs
6 tbsp melted Butter
2/3 c fresh or frozen (thawed) corn kernels
3 tbsp chopped Green Onions

Preheat oven to 350F and grease square baking pan or muffin pans.

Stir together flour, cornmeal, sugar, baking powder, salt and chili powder. Beat milk, eggs and butter into flour mixture until just blended. Fold in corn and green onions. Spoon batter into pan(s) and bake 40 to 50 minutes for one large pan or 20 to 25 minutes for individual muffins, or until center springs back when lightly pressed with fork. Cool in pan before removing. Serve warm with any main dish, or on their own.

The smell of cinnamon rolls baking for breakfast is sure to make even the tardiest late sleepers rouse themselves.

Cinnamon Rolls

2 c all-purpose Flour
2 tbsp Sugar
4 tsp Baking Powder
1 tsp Salt
1/4 c cool Butter
1/2 c Milk

Preheat oven to 400F.
Mix flour, sugar, baking powder and salt in large mixing bowl. Cut butter into mixture with pastry blender or two kitchen knives until mixture forms coarse crumbs. Gradually add milk to make a soft dough while mixing with a fork. Turn onto floured surface, knead gently, then roll into 12x8 inch rectangle. Set aside.

2/3 c soft Butter
2 c Brown Sugar, packed
2 tbsp Cinnamon
2/3 c Raisins

Cream together butter, sugar and cinnamon in mixing bowl. Drop spoonful of butter mixture into each of 12 large greased muffin pans. Spread remaining mixture over dough. Sprinkle on raisins. Roll up jelly-roll style. Cut into 12 equal slices. Place each in muffin pan. Bake 20 minutes or until browned. Remove from pans right away to avoid sticking. Serve warm.

Because pancakes can be sooo-o-o-o sweet, we like to serve them with something to cut the sweetness, like spicy sausages or thick cut back bacon.

Quilt Inn Pancakes

3 Eggs
2 c Buttermilk
1 1/2 c all-purpose Flour
1 tbsp Sugar
1 tsp Baking Soda
1/4 c Butter

Beat eggs with buttermilk in mixing bowl. Combine flour, sugar and baking powder. Stir together well. Mix dry ingredients into wet ingredients only until blended. Melt butter in skillet and stir into batter. Return skillet to high heat. Spoon 1/4 cup measures of batter into pan or onto griddle. Cook one side until small bubbles appear. Flip and cook other side. Repeat until all batter is used.

Serve with real maple syrup. If you like a strong maple flavour, look for Canadian maple syrup which has a thicker consistency and stronger maple taste. You will use less to achieve the same delicious taste, and save calories.

Muffins are popular breakfast fare at all times of the year. They also make great "pocket breakfasts" to take with you on an early morning walk. Here are some of our favourites.

Extra Bran Muffins

1 c whole wheat Flour
1 c all-purpose Flour
1/3 c Wheat Bran
1/3 c Oat Bran
1/3 c brown Sugar
1 tbsp Baking powder
1 tsp Cinnamon

1 Egg
1 c Milk
1/3 c melted Butter
2 tbsp Molasses
1/2 c Raisins
1/2 c Sesame seeds
1 c grated Carrots

Preheat oven to 400F

Sift together flours, brans, sugar, baking powder and cinnamon. Mix egg, milk, butter and molasses. Stir in raisins, seeds and carrots. Fold wet ingredients into dry ingredients until just blended. Do not overmix. Spoon mixture into greased muffin pans or paper cups. Bake for 25 minutes. Cool before removing from pan. Serve warm.

Banana Bran Cran Muffins

1 Egg
1 c mashed Banana
3/4 c Milk
1/3 c Brown Sugar
1/3 c vegetable Oil
1 1/2 c 100% Bran cereal
2 c all purpose Flour
1/2 c chopped Walnuts
1 tbsp Baking Powder
1/2 tsp Salt
1/2 tsp Cinnamon
3/4 c whole berry Cranberry Sauce

Preheat oven to 400F and grease 12 large muffin pans.

Combine egg, banana, milk, brown sugar and oil. Stir in bran cereal, and let stand 10 minutes. Mix remaining ingredients, except cranberry sauce, until just moistened. Spoon half the batter into muffin pans; top with cranberry sauce. Spoon remaining batter to cover cranberry sauce. Bake 20 to 25 minutes or until brown. Cool before removing from pan.

Hallowe'en Muffins

4 c all purpose Flour
1 tbsp Baking Powder
1 tbsp Cinnamon
2 tsp Baking Soda
1 tsp Ginger
1 tsp Nutmeg
1 tsp Salt
1/2 tsp Allspice
1/2 tsp Cloves
4 Eggs
1 can Pumpkin (14 oz)
1 c Apple juice
3/4 c melted Butter
1 1/2 c packed Brown Sugar
1 1/2 c chopped Pecans

Preheat oven to 375F and grease 24 muffin pans.

Stir together flour, baking powder, cinnamon, baking soda, and spices. In separate bowl, beat eggs, and mix in pumpkin, apple juice and butter. Blend in brown sugar. Blend wet ingredients into dry ingredients until just moistened. Fold in half the pecans. Spoon into greased muffin pans; sprinkle with remaining pecans. Bake for 25 minutes or until firm to the touch. Cool before removing from pan.

Cheesey Corn Muffins

These make a great luncheon roll served with soup.

1 2/3 c all purpose Flour
1 1/3 c Cornmeal
4 tsp Baking Powder
1 tsp Baking Soda
1 tsp Salt
2 Eggs
1 1/2 c Buttermilk

Quilt Inn Country Cookbook

1 can (14 oz) creamed corn
1/4 c melted Butter
1 1/2 c shredded Cheddar Cheese
Paprika to garnish

Preheat oven to 375F and grease 16 muffin pans.

Stir together flour, cornmeal, baking powder and soda, and salt. In separate bowl, beat eggs; blend in buttermilk, creamed corn and butter. Blend wet ingredients into dry ingredients. Sprinkle with 1 cup cheese and mix until moistened. Spoon into greased muffin pans. Sprinkle with remaining cheese. Dust with paprika. Bake for 25 minutes or until firm. Cool before removing from pans.

High Fiber "Good For You" Muffins

2 c all purpose Flour
1 1/2 c Raisins
1 c Muesli
1 c natural Bran
1 c packed Brown Sugar
2 tsp Baking Soda
1/2 tsp Salt
1 c plain Yogurt
1 c Milk
2/3 c vegetable Oil
1/4 c Molasses
2 tbsp rolled Oats

Preheat oven to 400F and grease 16 muffin pans.

Mix together flour, raisins, muesli, bran, sugar, soda and salt. In separate bowl, blend yogurt, milk, oil and molasses. Mix wet ingredients into dry until just moistened. Spoon batter into muffin pans, or paper-lined cups. Bake for 20 minutes or until firm to touch. Cool before removing from pans.

Aliske Webb

Zesty Orange Muffins

2 c all-purpose Flour
1/2 c Sugar
2 tsp Baking powder
1 tsp Baking soda
1/4 tsp Salt
1/3 c Currants (or dried chopped apricots)
1 Egg
1 c plain Yogurt
1/4 c melted Butter
2 tbsp Orange rind strips, chopped fine
1/4 c Orange juice

Preheat oven to 350F and grease muffin pans.

Stir together flour, sugar, baking powder, baking soda and salt in large mixing bowl. Mix in currants. In another bowl beat egg; blend in yogurt, butter, orange rind and juice. Stir into flour mixture and blend only until dry ingredients are moistened. Spoon into muffin pans. Bake for 20-25 minutes, (depending on size of muffin pans) or until firm to touch.

Cheesecake Muffins

Filling:
1 pkg Cream cheese, softened
2 tbsp Sugar
1 tsp Orange rind, grated fine

Cream cheese, sugar and orange rind together in bowl until smooth. Set aside.

Batter:
1 1/4 c all-purpose Flour
1 tsp Baking powder
1/3 c Butter
1/2 c brown Sugar
2 Eggs

2 tbsp Orange juice concentrate
1 tsp Orange rind, grated
1/2 c evaporated Milk
1 1/4 c finely grated Carrots
1./2 c Raisins
1/2 c Walnuts, chopped
1 tsp Cinnamon

Preheat oven to 350F

Cream butter and brown sugar together in mixing bowl. Beat in eggs, orange juice concentrate and milk. Stir in orange rind, carrots, raisins and walnuts.

Combine flour, baking powder and cinnamon in large mixing bowl. Add wet mixture. Stir just until moistened. Spoon 2 tablespoon batter into each muffin cup, using only half the batter mix. Spoon 1 tablespoon filling on top. Cover with remaining batter. Bake for 15-20 minutes or until top is firm and springs back when pressed lightly.

Bill Parker brought us this recipe from the Bon Ton Restaurant in New Orleans, where it's a popular dish with the locals .

Bread Pudding with Jack Daniel's Sauce

Pudding:
3/4 c Sugar
2 c Milk
2 Eggs
1 tsp real Vanilla
1/4 c Raisins
6 c cubed French bread

Preheat oven to 325F and grease a loaf pan.

In large bowl, whisk together sugar, eggs, milk and vanilla until fluffy. Stir in raisins and bread. Let soak for 20 minutes, stirring occasionally. Pack mixture lightly into loaf pan.

Place loaf pan in larger pan of hot water to prevent burning. Bake 1 hour, 15 minutes or until lightly brown and set.

Jack Daniel's Sauce:

1/4 lb Butter
1 c Sugar
1/4 c 10% Cream
1 Egg
6 tbsp Jack Daniel's bourbon (no substitutions)

Mix butter, sugar and cream in top of double boiler. Cook over simmering water until sugar dissolves and mixture is hot. Whisk in egg and continue cooking until sauce thickens slightly. Stir in bourbon.

To serve: Slice pudding, pour sauce over it and garnish with berries in season.

Adam's Search For The Ultimate Rib

We have travelled all across North America, searching for the ultimate rib. Surprisingly, there are many others who have also embarked on this culinary quest. In fact, if you mention to someone that you are a "rib freak", they are just as likely to tell you about their favorite restaurant, recipe, or sauce. We even have a friend, Gerry, who collects jars of sauces: some people have wine cellars, but there's our Ger, down in his basement late at night, applying a quarter turn to each dusty bottle -- to keep the lid wet, naturally.

Ribs differ wherever you go. Some people prefer pork ribs, the side variety for thinness, baby backs for meaty, sweet flavor, country style for thick pleasure, or sweet and sour cuts. Others swear by beef ribs, from the full bone of the standing rib roast to the short rib type.

And then there's the sauce. Ah sauce! Ketchup-based, mustard-enhanced, garlicked, honeyed, hickory-smoked, hot, medium, sweet, or no sauce at all. The varieties are as endless as the rib afficianados who swear by them.

Many of the commercially prepared sauces rely on an ingredient called "liquid smoke" to give a hickory flavor to the sauce. Liquid smoke was first commercially prepared in Nebraska in 1895, originally from the tar of burned wood that was dissolved in water (boy, does that ever sound good!). Nowadays, it is synthetically produced and the unhealthy tars and resins have been removed. Because it is concentrated, a very small amount of this ingredient goes a long, long way and can easily overpower other more subtle flavors. For some, hickory smoke is an acquired taste, and should never stand in the way of enjoying ribs, your way.

And so, once committed to the rib quest, one needs to search out, in every eating establishment, the "rib dinners" on the menu. However, for the true, and venturesome, connaisseur, it's simply a matter of saying, without even opening the menu, "I'll have the ribs, please."

We have eaten ribs in franchise-type restaurants, in

smoky beer joints, in specialty places where the ribs are smoked in a pit, or baked in a brick oven for up to 24 hours. Naturally, we think those at the Quilt Inn are the best. But the joy of the quest is that it is never-ending. Oh, rapture!

The best rib story that I can think of, I owe to Alan Alda in his role of "Hawkeye Pierce" on the long-running (still re-running) television series, M*A*S*H. During this memorable episode, Hawkeye has had two weeks of liver and fish, and he's had enough. As he says, "I've eaten a river of liver and an ocean of fish, and I won't take it any longer!" What's the answer. "Ribs", he says to his partner in crime, "Trapper John" McIntyre. "But not just any ribs. They have to be 'Adam's Ribs'. With sauce. And coleslaw... From Chicago!" Their bounty is shipped all the way to Korea marked "medical supplies", and after a number of comic mishaps, finally arrive. Was it worth it? Any rib-lover watching the episode would say YES! We couldn't understand why anyone would think it an unreasonable request, or quest, at all. The search for the ultimate rib goes on. It knows no boundaries!

***

There are as many ways to cook ribs at home as there are sauces to cook them in: boil to tenderize, marinate or not, bake, broil, barbecue. I think we've tried them all and here are the best of the ones we like to prepare.

Hot Dijon Ribs

4 lbs pork Spareribs
1 c liquid Honey
3/4 c Dijon Mustard
2 to 3 tbsp Hot sauce
1 tbsp Soya sauce
2 tsp Onion powder
1/2 tsp Garlic powder

Cut ribs into serving size pieces. Place in large saucepan, cover with water. Bring to boil. Reduce heat, cover and simmer for 1 hour or until meat is tender. Drain ribs. Set aside.

Sauce: Combine all ingredients. Broil or barbecue ribs for 10 minutes, until brown. Baste with sauce on both sides. Cook another 5 minutes per side. Serve with baked beans, coleslaw and lots of paper napkins!

Michael's Baked Beans

These are traditional in many parts of the country, as the delightful accompaniment to ribs. How are they prepared?

1 large can of commercial baked beans *(make it easy on yourself!)*
1 tbsp dry mustard
1 handful brown sugar
3 glugs maple syrup

Mix. Heat. Eat!

Honey Garlic Baked Ribs

6 lb back or side ribs
3 tbsp Garlic powder
3 tbsp fresh ground Pepper
3 tsp Oregano
1 tsp Thyme
Salt to taste

Preheat oven to 400F

Place ribs in large pot. Cover with water and add other ingredients. Bring to boil. Simmer 10 minutes.

Remove from heat and let cool for 1 hour in liquid.

Sauce:
2 c liquid Honey
2 tbsp Molasses
1/2 c Chinese Plum sauce
1/2 c Steak sauce
3 tbsp white Wine
2 tbsp Garlic powder
2 tsp dry Mustard
2 tbsp fresh ground Pepper
2 tbsp Worcestershire sauce
2 tbsp Vinegar
2 tbsp Soya sauce

Mix all sauce ingredients together well. Remove ribs from liquid and place on broiler rack. Brush with sauce and bake until browned on both sides, (15 minutes). Serve with remaining sauce.

Sweet and Sour Broiled Spareribs

4 lb lean Spareribs
2 Onions, chopped
1/3 c Brown Sugar
1/2 c Vinegar
1 tbsp Soya sauce
1/2 c Pineapple juice
1/3 c Water
1/2 tsp Salt
1/4 tsp fresh ground Pepper
1 tbsp Cornstarch

Place ribs on broiler pan. Sprinkle with salt and pepper. Broil until deep brown on both sides.

Saute onions in deep pot until softened. Add all other ingredients, except cornstarch. Add ribs. Cover pot and simmer over low for 2 hours.

Remove ribs. Make paste with cornstarch and spoonful of water. Thicken sauce with cornstarch paste. Return ribs to sauce. Transfer to serving dish and serve with Petit Sirah wine.

Very Merry Baked Ribs

5 lb pork Ribs
Salt and fresh ground Pepper to taste
1 c sweet red Vermouth *(Cinzano works well)*

Preheat oven to 350F

Rub salt and pepper into ribs and place in baking pan. Cover loosely with foil and baker for 30 minutes. Turn and bake another 30 minutes.

Pour vermouth over ribs, basting every 15 minutes and turning, and bake uncovered for another hour.

Beer and Honey Marinated Ribs

8 lb Spareribs
3 c Beer
1 c Honey
2 tbsp Lemon juice
2 tsp Chili powder
2 tsp Sage
1 1/2 tsp dry Mustard
1/2 tsp Salt

Place ribs in large pan. Mix all other ingredients and pour over ribs. Let stand overnight in refrigerator, turning occasionally. Remove ribs from marinade, reserve liquid.

Broil or barbecue ribs on medium-low heat for 1 hour, brushing with marinade. Or, bake in 350F oven for 1 1/2 hours.

We happened to be in Washington, D.C. on a business trip, and you would have thought that with all the five-star restaurants in the area, the culinary world would have been at our feet. Well, not us: we had to travel 50 miles to a place we had heard of called Dirty Pete's Ribs, serving on the weekends only. Neither Pete nor his daughter-in-law, Carole, would reveal the secrets of his sauce, but both agreed that what was required was slo-o-o-o-w cooking. I think the secret to Pete's Sauce was Jack Daniel's (whether it was in Pete or the sauce, I'm not too sure). Perhaps you'll have the opportunity to visit. If so, say "hi" from us, and set a spell at the picnic tables in the back.

Hickory Smoked Barbecue Ribs

2 slabs baby back ribs or Spareribs
1/2 tsp Cinnamon
1/2 tsp ground Cloves
1/4 tsp Pepper
1 c Hickory wood chips
Barbecue sauce

Preheat oven to 400F

Rub cinnamon, cloves and pepper into both sides of ribs. Place ribs on wire rack on baking pan. Cover with foil. Bake for 3 hours, until tender.

Wrap hickory wood chips in aluminium foil, pierce foil to allow smoke to escape, and place directly in the center of hot barbecue coals.

Baste ribs and place on grill above wood chips. Cover grill and cook 10 minutes. Turn ribs, baste again and cook another 10 minutes or until ribs are browned but still moist. Serve with a hearty Beaujolais wine.

Not Pete's Barbecue Sauce:

2 15-oz cans Tomato sauce
1/2 c Molasses
10 cloves Garlic
2 tbsp ground Cumin
2 tbsp dry Mustard
Fresh ground Pepper
1/2 tsp Cinnamon
1/4 tsp Anise seed
1/4 tsp hot Pepper flakes
1/2 c red wine Vinegar

Combine all ingredients except vinegar in saucepan. Simmer, covered, on low heat for 1 hour, stirring occasionally. Add vinegar to taste and simmer for another 15 minutes. Chill at least 24 hours, until ready to use.

Grown-up Ribs

4 to 5 lb meaty pork ribs

Rib Sauce:
1 Onion, chopped
4 cloves Garlic, chopped
1 Tomato, seeded and chopped
1/2 sweet red Pepper, chopped
1/2 tsp Salt
1/2 tsp fresh ground Pepper
1/2 tsp Paprika
1/4 tsp Turmeric
1/3 c brown Sugar
1/2 c Beer *(for young 'uns Ribs, substitute Coke or Dr Pepper for beer)*
1/4 c apple cider Vinegar
1 tbsp Worcestershire sauce
1/4 tsp Hot sauce *(Tabasco will do)*

Combine all ingredients in blender and process until smooth. Place ribs in deep dish and pour sauce over ribs. Marinate for 3 hours.

Preheat grill.

Transfer ribs to 2 sheets of heavy-duty aluminium foil. Fold up edges, pour 1/2 cup marinade over ribs. Seal foil edges together. Place foil-wrapped ribs on grill, cover and cook for 2 hours.

Ten minutes before serving, remove ribs from foil and grill over medium heat for 5 minutes per side, basting with sauce.

And while you have the barbecue on, you might as well cook some vegetables too. For each person, chop one potato and half an onion into large chunks. Place on 1' square of heavy-duty aluminium foil; sprinkle on your favorite savory spice mix, or simply grind fresh pepper over the vegetables. Add a dollup of butter, or margarine if you are health-conscious. Fold over the foil, sealing the ends, and place on cooler part of grill. Cook for 20 minutes, turning frequently to prevent burning. Serve with lots of napkins. Try this with fresh asparagus, or any other combination of "solid" vegetables.

Creole Ribs

2 lb pork Spareribs
1 Onion, chopped
1 green Pepper, seeded and chopped
1/2 c green Onion, chopped
1/2 c fresh Parsley, chopped
2 c Rice, uncooked
1 tsp Salt
1/2 tsp fresh ground Pepper
1/4 c vegetable Oil

Brown ribs in oil in large deep skillet. Remove and drain well on paper towels. Reserve drippings in pan and saute onion, green pepper and green onion for 2 minutes. Return ribs to pan. Add remaining ingredients and water to cover. Cover and simmer for 1 hour or until ribs are tender and rice is cooked. Try these with a light Gewurtraminer wine.

Mediterranean Short Ribs

6 lb beef Shortribs
1/4 c Olive oil
1 can plum Tomatoes, drained and chopped
1 Onion, sliced
1/2 c dry red Wine
1/2 c beef Stock
6 cloves Garlic, minced
4 tbsp fresh Parsley, chopped
2 tsp fresh Rosemary, chopped
1/2 tsp ground Cinnamon
2 tsp fresh ground Pepper

Preheat oven to 350F

Mix tomatoes, stock, garlic, parsley, rosemary and cinnamon together in a bowl. Set aside.

Brown shortribs in olive oil over medium heat. Place in roasting pan and sprinkle with pepper. Saute onion in shortrib browning until tender. Add to shortribs. Add wine to skillet and bring to a boil, deglazing pan. Add liquid browning to shortribs.

Pour tomato mixture over ribs and mix well. Cover and bake for 2 1/2 hours. Uncover pan and cook another 20 minutes to reduce liquid. Skim off any grease. Serve with wild rice sidedish.

For something completely different, try...

Stuffed Ribs

2 full racks of ribs

Stuffing:
1 Onion, chopped
1/4 c Celery, chopped
2 tbsp Butter
1 c cooked mashed Potatoes
1/2 c Breadcrumbs
1 Egg, beaten
1/4 tsp fresh Parsley, chopped
1/4 tsp Marjoram
1/4 tsp Salt
Fresh ground Pepper to taste

Saute onion and celery in butter until tender. Stir in potatoes, breadcrumbs, egg, parsley, marjoram, salt and pepper. Mix well.

Place rack of ribs on greased, shallow roasting pan. Spoon stuffing on one rack of ribs. Cover with remaining rack. Tie or secure with string. Rub ribs with fresh ground Pepper and sage.

Bake at 475F, uncovered for 20 minutes. Reduce heat to 325F, Cover. Bake for 1 hour or until tender. Cut between rib sections for individual servings and serve with Beaujolais wine.

Alternative Stuffing:
1 c Breadcrumbs
1/2 c Onion, chopped fine
1 c Apples, chopped fine
1 tbsp brown Sugar
1/2 tsp Salt
1/2 tsp fresh ground Pepper

Combine all ingredients and use as above.

Quilt Inn Country Cookbook

Everyone, and every region, has their own distinctive and unique barbecue sauce recipe. Here are some of our favorites. It's great to have a specialty, but we like to prepare different sauces at different times, just to keep guests interested, trying to identify "what IS that ingredient I can taste?".

Southern Style Barbecue Sauce

1 c Peach preserves
1 Onion, chopped fine
1 tbsp tomato sauce
1/3 c brown Sugar
1/2 cider Vinegar
1 tsp Paprika
2 tsp dry Mustard
1/4 tsp Hot sauce *(Tabasco will do)*
2 tbsp Worcestershire sauce

Combine all ingredients in a saucepan. Bring to a boil, reduce heat. Simmer uncovered for 10 minutes. Chill until ready to use.

Racetrack Barbecue Sauce

Serve on Derby Day with Mint Juleps

1 Onion, chopped
1 c Ketchup
1/2 c Vinegar
1 c Water
1 tbsp Horseradish
1 tbsp Mustard
1 tbsp fresh Parsley, chopped
1 tbsp brown Sugar
1 tsp fresh ground Pepper

Combine all ingredients in saucepan. Bring to a boil, while stirring well. Reduce heat and simmer, uncovered for 15 minutes, stirring occasionally. Chill until ready to use.

Aliske Webb

Molasses Sauce

1/2 c Molasses
1/2 c cider Vinegar
1/2 c Onion, chopped
1/2 c Mustard
Juice of 2 Lemons
Zest of 2 Lemons
1 tsp Hot sauce (Tabasco will do)
1/2 tsp Salt
1/2 tsp Garlic powder
1/2 tsp fresh ground Pepper

Combine all ingredients in a saucepan. Bring to a boil, reduce heat, cover and simmer for 10 minutes. Refrigerate until ready to use.

To the Manor Born Barbecue Sauce

1/2 c Sherry
1/4 c Ketchup
1 tbsp brown Sugar
1 tbsp white wine Vinegar
1 tbsp Worcestershire sauce
1/2 tsp Salt
1/2 tsp fresh ground Pepper
1/8 tsp Chili pepper

Combine all ingredients in a saucepan. Bring to a boil, reduce heat and simmer for 5 minutes. Refrigerate until ready to use.

Yuppie Barbecue Sauce

1/2 c dried Apricots
Water to cover
1 green Onion, chopped
3 tbsp vegetable oil

1/2 c raspberry Vinegar *(or other fancy vinegar)*
1/4 c liquid Honey
1 tsp Soya sauce
1/4 c Tomato sauce
1/2 tsp Oregano
1/4 tsp Salt
Fresh ground Pepper to taste

Cover apricots with water in saucepan. Bring to boil, reduce heat. Simmer until tender (1/2 hour). Cool.

Place apricots and 1/2 cup of the liquid in blender. Process until smooth. Add other ingredients and pour into saucepan. Bring to boil, reduce heat. Simmer 5 minutes. Chill until ready to use.

Oriental Baked Ribs

2 racks of spareribs

4 cloves Garlic, minced
4 tbsp Ketchup
4 tbsp Soy sauce
4 tbsp Hoisin sauce
4 tbsp dry Sherry
2 tbsp fresh Ginger, grated
2 tbsp Honey

Preheat oven to 300F and cut ribs into individual ribs and arrange in shallow baking pan. Bake for 45 minutes.

Combine remaining ingredients and brush spareribs lightly. Bake additional 30 minutes and turn. Brush with more sauce and bake another 30 minutes or until nicely browned.

Some people like to marinate their ribs overnight first to tenderize and flavorize them before grilling. The marinade is then used to baste the ribs during cooking.

Ginger Marinade

2 green Onions, chopped
2 tbsp Sesame seeds, toasted
6 tbsp Soya sauce
6 cloves Garlic, minced
2 tsp fresh Ginger root, grated
2 tbsp Sugar
2 tbsp Peanut oil

Combine all ingredients in a bowl. Pour over ribs.

Tandoori Marinade

1/2 c Yogurt, plain
4 cloves Garlic, chopped
1 tsp fresh Ginger root, grated
2 tbsp Lemon juice
2 tbsp Lime juice
1/2 tsp Salt
1/2 tsp Cumin seeds
1/2 tsp ground Coriander
1/4 tsp Turmeric
1/4 tsp Cayenne pepper
1/4 tsp fresh ground Pepper
1/4 tsp ground Cinnamon
Pinch of Cloves

Pour lemon and lime juice over ribs, coating well. Combine all other ingredients in blender and process until smooth.

California Marinade

1 c Orange juice
1/4 c liquid Honey
1/4 c Vinegar
2 tsp Zest of Orange

Combine all ingredients in bowl and rub over ribs, coating thoroughly.

Tex Mex Marinade

2 c Bloody Mary mix
Juice of 1 Lemon
2 tbsp Horseradish
2 tbsp Dijon Mustard
5 tbsp mild Chilis, chopped fine
1 tsp fresh ground Pepper

Combine all ingredients in bowl and pour over ribs.

Lemon Baster

1/2 c Lemon juice
1 c Olive oil
4 cloves Garlic, minced
1/8 tsp Oregano, crushed
1 tsp Lemon zest, grated
Salt and fresh ground Pepper to taste

Combine all ingredients in bowl and baste ribs while cooking.

And, when you can't think of anything else to do with ribs, you can always make soup...

Shortrib Soup

4 lb beef Shortribs, cut in chunks
1 Onion, sliced
4 c beef Stock
3 Celery stalks, chopped
3 Carrots, chopped
1 Leek, chopped
1 c Mushrooms, sliced
2 tbsp Parsley, chopped
1 tbsp fresh Dill, chopped
Salt and fresh ground Pepper to taste

Place ribs and onions in soup pot. Add stock to cover and bring to a boil. Reduce heat and cover. Simmer for 2 hours or until tender, skimming off fat occasionally.

Remove ribs and remove meat from bones, discard bones. Set meat aside.

Chill broth until fat rises to surface and skim off. Strain broth, if desired, and return to pot. Return to heat. Add celery, carrots, mushrooms and leeks. Cook for 2 minutes. Add meat. Stir in parsley, dill, salt and pepper. Heat thoroughly and serve with a full-bodied Chardonnay wine.

Sittin' Loose

Edna Mae, one of my Grama's oldest friends, worked hard on a farm all day, and in the evening you could find her flopped in a comfortable old rocking chair on the front porch. Her favorite expression for her feeling at that time of day was, "When ah sits, ah sits loose!" Now there's a country inn attitude for you -- learn to sit loose.

The important thing about a country inn is to have lots of favourite places to sit. Each one needs to be different and inviting, yet has to make the sitter feel that they are the first to have found this particular spot, with this special outview on the world, or that unusual insight into life. If you need lessons on finding favourite spots around an inn, find one of the inn cats. They know the best places and they usually don't mind a little, if quiet, company. We have several cats and lots of places.

You need to find, however, the cat whose personality matches your sittin' mood. Now, Nine Patch, for example, our long hair calico cat, is built for comfort, not speed. Michael says that from behind she looks like a hairy bowling ball with a tail. A true "Garfield" of cats, you see her ambling slowly around the place, examining every blade of grass, like a reincarnated Sixties hippie on bad drugs, and blinking sleepily through half-open eyes. Nine Patch looks for comfort, and she usually dozes on a cozy quilt-covered chair on the veranda out of the wind, in a sunny windowseat or behind the orchard wall on a warm stone slab. Her places are warm and cozy and sleep-inducing. If you're in a mellow mood, follow Nine Patch, and take a book only if you don't intend to read it.

Dixie on the other hand, is a gadabout cat. A fluffy brainless grey and white furball, she's the kind of cat that starts to purr as soon as she walks into a room, as if announcing, "OK everyone, I'm here and I'm looking for love." She purrs if you just look at her from across a room. Dixie pays no particular mind to comfort; she'll sleep anywhere, anytime, no matter how lumpy it is, so long as there are people about, or the potential of people about. Quite foolishly, she'll sleep in doorways, busy doorways at that, waiting to make sure she's there to catch any tidbits of conversation, or food, and often getting stepped on. Follow her to the places where people gather to chat: the main room by the fireplace, the stone patio, around the kitchen table. Don't be surprised if she follows you to your room at night for some bedside conversation.

Then there's little Hobbes. A small sleek short-haired cat with grey stripey pyjamas. She's a little skittish, shy and hard to find. Her places are quiet unobtrusive spots to sit and watch the world, without being seen watching. They're philosophical, often elevated and hard to reach places. Least visited, most treasured. The loft in the barn by the window overlooking the courtyard; top of the bookshelf; behind the lattice under the veranda. Awkward, I agree. You may have to find your own Hobbes-like places where you can be alert, watchful and contemplative.

Or, like Edna Mae, you can just "sit loose" in a wicker chair or rocking chair on the long verandah that runs across the front of the Inn.

※ ※ ※

Picnic fare goes well with good sittin' places. At the Quilt Inn, many guests like to go off by themselves and enjoy space, quiet contemplation and alfresco dining. We pack picnic lunches. (Tuna fish for Nine Patch, Dixie, or Hobbes is optional). Grab a cat and go!

Speaking of cats, Gracie Allen was once asked by a fellow cat-lover: "How do you raise your cats?" Gracie shrugged: "Two hands under the belly, and lift!"

Angela's Summer Seafood Salad

1/2 lb Shrimp, shelled and deveined *(Angela, one of our cooks, is obsessive about deveining and cleaning shrimp: the "vein" is actually the shrimp's intestine)*
1/2 lb Scallops, halved
2 tbsp Olive Oil
1 Onion, chopped fine
2 c long grain Rice
3 c Chicken stock
1/2 tsp Salt
1/2 tsp fresh ground Pepper
1 c roasted red Peppers, chopped fine
4 green Onions, chopped fine
1 1/2 c green Peas (thawed, if frozen)

Heat oil for 1 minute in saucepan. Add onion and saute for 2 minutes or until slightly soft. Stir in rice, add stock, salt and pepper. Bring to boil. Reduce heat, simmer covered for 10 minutes. Stir in roasted red peppers, green onions, peas. Cover, cook for 2 minutes. Remove from heat and let stand, covered, for 5 minutes.

Dressing:
1/4 c Olive Oil
3 tbsp Lemon juice
2 tbsp Balsamic or red wine Vinegar
1/4 c fresh Dill, chopped
1 tsp Dijon Mustard

Whisk lemon juice with vinegar and mustard until smooth. Add oil while whisking vigorously. Stir in dill. Transfer shrimp and scallop mixture to large bowl. Pour dressing over, toss well. Chill and serve. Garnish with slices of Spanish onions. Serve with a chilled Chenin Blanc wine.

Pocket Pita Pooches

6 small Pita bread
2 c left-over cold meat, ham or corned beef, ground
1 c sharp Cheddar cheese, shredded
2 hard-boiled Eggs, chopped
1/2 c green Onion, chopped fine
4 tbsp Mayonnaise
1/2 c Chili sauce

Preheat oven to 450 or heat barbeque to medium heat.
Mix together meat, cheese, eggs and onions. Stir in mayonnaise and chili sauce. Cut off top edge of pita and open by sliding knife between the two layers of bread. Spoon mixture into pitas. Wrap loosely in foil and bake for 15 minutes. Serve with raw carrot sticks.

Pocket Pita Pooches Encore

6 Pita bread
1 ripe Avocado
2 ripe Tomatoes
6 strips Bacon, cooked crisp
Bean sprouts
Mayonnaise

Cut off top edge of pita bread, open with knife between the two layers of bread. Dice tomato and avocado, crumble bacon, mix together with bean sprouts. Add enough mayonnaise to moisten. Spoon mixture into pita, wrap in foil. Pack in picnic hamper with crisp apples.

Classic Caesar Salad

1 head Romaine lettuce
4 slices Bacon, cooked crisp and diced
1 c Croutons
1/2 c Parmesan cheese

Dressing:
1/3 c Olive oil
1/3 c red wine Vinegar
1 tsp Anchovy paste
1/4 tsp Tabasco sauce
1 tsp Worcestershire sauce
1 tbsp dry Mustard
3 cloves Garlic, crushed
2 tbsp Flour
2 c Milk
2 Egg yolks
Salt and fresh ground Pepper to taste

Combine mustard, flour, salt and peper in top of double boiler. Stir in milk. Beat in egg yolks. Simmer over gently boiling water until mixture thickens. Remove from heat. Stir in Worcestershire, Tabasco, garlic, anchovy paste, vinegar and oil. Mix well. Chill until ready to serve.

Wash and dry lettuce. Break into pieces. Toss with dressing to coat leaves. Sprinkle with bacon and croutons and cheese. Toss lightly again. Serve with red Zinfandel wine.

Curried Salad

6 cups mixed garden vegetables (try celery slices, carrot strips, cauliflower, green and red peppers, turnip strips)

Steam vegetables for 5 minutes. Drain and cool.

Dressing:
1/2 c white Vinegar
1/4 c Sugar
1/4 c Salad oil
1/4 tsp Salt
1/2 tsp fresh ground Pepper
2 tsp Curry powder

Mix all ingredients well and pour over vegetables. Let chill overnight in refrigerator.

Aliske Webb

Rice Salad

3 c cold cooked Rice
1/2 c cooked Peas
1/2 c cooked corn
1/2 c Raisins
1/2 c red and green Pepper, chopped
1/3 c Olive oil
6 slices bacon, cooked crisp and crumbled
Salt and fresh ground Pepper to taste

Combine all ingredients in a bowl. Toss with olive oil and chill overnight in refrigerator before serving. Garnish with orange sections.

(If you like to plan your meals in advance, this is a good dish to plan for a picnic the day after you serve fresh cooked corn, peas or rice for dinner.)

Chicken Salad

3 lb boneless Chicken, cut in chunks
1 1/2 c Pecan halves
1 c Celery, diced
1 1/2 c Sour cream
1 1/2 c Mayonnaise
3 c Water
1 chicken Bouillon cube
1 lb green seedless grapes
1 tsp fresh Dill
Salt and fresh ground Pepper to taste

Preheat oven to 350F and place chicken in shallow pan.

Bring water to boil, add bouillon cube. Bring to boil. Pour over chicken to cover. Cover and bake 30 minutes or until cooked thoroughly. Chill in liquid, then drain and discard liquid.

Shred chicken into pieces in large bowl. Add grapes, pecans, celery and dill. Toss well. Mix sour cream and mayonnaise in mixing bowl. Toss with chicken mixture. Season to taste. Cover and chill before serving. Serve on bed of lettuce, garnish with cherry tomatoes cut in half. Serve with white Vouvray wine.

Northern California Salad

1 head Romaine lettuce
Alfalfa sprouts
1 Orange, peeled and sectioned
4 green Onions, chopped
1/2 green Olives with pimiento, sliced
2 c Cauliflower florets

Dressing:
1/2 c Olive oil
1/2 c wine Vinegar
Zest of 1 Orange
1/4 c Orange juice
1 tsp fresh Basil
1 tsp fresh ground Pepper
Salt

Combine all ingredients and blend well. Pour over cauliflower, onions and olives, marinate for 4 hours. Before serving toss with lettuce, sprouts and orange sections. Serve with white Zinfandel wine.

Southern California Salad

1/2 head Romaine lettuce
1/2 head Iceberg lettuce
1/2 lb Spinach
1 tin Mandarin oranges, drained
1/2 c toasted Almond slivers

Wash and dry lettuce. Drain oranges. Toast almonds. Mix in bowl and set aside.

Dressing:
1/2 c Salad oil
1/4 c wine Vinegar (or try any flavored vinegar such as Raspberry vinegar)
1/4 tsp Salt
Fresh ground pepper to taste
Dash of Tabasco sauce
1 tbsp Parsley

Combine all ingredients and blend well. Chill until serving. Just before serving toss greens, oranges and almonds with dressing. Serve with chilled white Zinfandel wine.

Practically Perfect Potato Salad

6 to 10 Potatoes, boiled, cooled and cut in chunks
3 hard-boiled Eggs, chopped
1/2 lb Salami, Ham, or other favorite deli meat, cut into chunks
3 Dill pickles, chopped
1 Onion, chopped
2 Apples, cored and chopped
3 tbsp Mayonnaise
3 tbsp red wine Vinegar
Salt and fresh ground Pepper to taste
Paprika

Mix potatoes, eggs, pickles, apple and onion in large bowl. Fry salami lightly and drain off excess fat, cool. Stir salami, mayonnaise and seasoning into potato mixture. Chill for 2 hours before serving. Garnish with slivered red and green sweet peppers. Serve with a robust Bordeaux wine.

Lo-Cal Potato Salad

3 lb red Potatoes
4 green Onions, sliced thin
1 red Onion, sliced thin
1/2 c black Olives, drained

Salt and Pepper to taste

Scrub potatoes, cut into chunks, cook until tender. Drain well. Combine with green onions, red onions and olives. Set aside.

Dressing:
2 c Milk
3 Egg yolks
3 tbsp Vinegar
1 tsp Salt
2 tsp dry Mustard
2 tbsp brown Sugar
3 tbsp Butter
2 tbsp all-purpose Flour
1 tsp Horseradish
1 tbsp Dijon Mustard
Pinch Cayenne Pepper

Combine salt, mustard, sugar, flour and cayenne in top of double boiler. Add milk and egg yolk. Stir until smooth. Cook over boiling water, or medium heat, until thickened. Stir in butter and vinegar. Chill. Stir horseradish and mustard into dressing. Season to taste. Toss over potato mixture, coating thoroughly. Serve chilled. Garnish with cucumber slices.

Crab Salad

1 head Boston lettuce
1 lb fresh Crabmeat
Juice of 1/2 Lemon
Zest of 1/2 Lemon
2 stalks Celery, diced fine
1/2 c Mayonnaise
2 tbsp fresh Chives, chopped
Lemon wedges for garnish

Gently mix together crabmeat, lemon juice and zest, celery, mayonnaise and chives. Serve with a crisp Reisling wine.

Make a bed of lettuce leaves on 4 individual plates. Spoon crab mixture onto lettuce. Garnish with lemon wedges. Serve with chilled white Zinfandel wine.

Crazy Quilt Fruit Salad

4 seedless Oranges, sectioned
1/2 fresh Pineapple, diced
2 sweet Apples, cored and diced
1 Banana, sliced
1 Kiwi fruit, sliced
1 c fresh Strawberries, halved
1/2 pint whipping Cream
1 oz Cointreau *(or other orange flavor liqueur)*
1/2 pint Mayonnaise
1 head Boston lettuce

Gently mix all fruit together. Whip cream. Mix liqueur into mayonnaise and then gently fold mayonnaise into whipped cream. Add cream mixture to fruit.

Arrange lettuce on 4 individual salad plates. Spoon fruit onto lettuce and serve.

Tomatoware Tomato-fare

I've been haunting antique shows, shops and flea markets for years. Which is why The Inn is filled with an eclectic mix of antique furniture and bizarre collections. I'm always on the lookout for that fabulous $10 unrecognized treasure. Happily, I've found a couple. Like a gambler convinced a big win is at hand, I'm hooked on bargain hunting. I've also outsmarted myself on occasion, by being part-smart about antiques. Caveat emptor. Antique dealers are seldom as dumb as we would like to think they are. If something is that cheap, it's probably a fake -- you're the only one who doesn't know it.

The first time I remember seeing "tomatoware", I laughed at the idea of making dishes, teapots, cream and sugars, and so forth, to look like something so mundane as a tomato. Who would buy that, I said to Michael, and we scoffed. I would never buy anything that gaudy, I said smugly. Well, as my wise old Grama used to say, "never say 'never', you just never know..." Check out the front cover of this book. Yes, that's our Chatham cupboard, circa 1900, and (part) of our tomatoware collection, circa 1907. The Chatham was a contemporary of the Hoosier cupboard, and it stands in the summer kitchen that was converted into an informal family diningroom.

You see, we kept seeing it everywhere. We kept laughing at it. Until we finally had to buy some because it was, well, bizarre. And after all, it was cheap. That was a few hundred dollars ago!

Once we were committed to ownership, we did some research. We found out that there are several nationalities of tomatoware. Surprisingly, the Italians don't make tomatoware -- too busy with the original fruit, I suppose. The most expensive is Bayreuth, made of fine china in Germany. Then there is cheap and cheerful American pottery tomatoware. And finally there is knock-off Japanese pottery. Of course, now that we specialize, we only collect the Occupied-Japan-era tomatoware!

At least I stopped laughing at it. (I think it's started to laugh at me. Note the teapot on the cover.) And I learned a whole lot more about antiques in the process. The stuff has grown on me. Every year we have a tomato weekend to celebrate the lowly vegetable, or fruit to be more exact. We set a completely green and red table with all our tomatoware plates and cups and saucers and serving dishes. Here are some of our favorite tomato-fare recipes that we serve on Tomato Weekend at The Quilt Inn.

* * *

Cool Tomato Soup

2 tbsp Olive Oil
1 Onion, chopped
3 c Tomatoes, peeled and seeded
1 c Chicken stock
1 tbsp Lemon juice
1 c Yogurt, plain
2 tbsp fresh Parsley, chopped
2 tbsp fresh Basil, chopped
1/2 tsp Salt
1/4 tsp fresh ground Pepper

Heat oil over medium heat in saucepan. Cook onion for 3-4 minutes or until soft. Add tomatoes and cook for 2 minutes. Pour in stock, bring to boil over high heat. Lower heat and simmer, covered for 10 minutes or until tomatoes are tender. Let cool.

In blender, blend tomato mixture until smooth. Add lemon juice. Whisk yogurt in mixing bowl until smooth, whisk into tomato mixture. Whisk in parsley, basil, salt and pepper. Serve chilled, garnish with swirl of yogurt.

Fried Red Tomatoes

3 ripe Tomatoes
1/3 c Olive Oil
4 cloves Garlic, minced
1 tbsp chopped fresh Thyme
1/4 tsp hot Pepper flakes
2 tbsp fresh Parsley, chopped
1/2 tsp Salt

Core tomatoes and cut into 1/2 inch slices. Dry with paper towel.

Heat oil over low heat in skillet. Cook garlic, thyme and pepper flakes for 2 minutes or until fragrant. Cook tomatoes, one layer at a time, for 3 to 5 minutes per side or until they just start to soften. Drain with slotted spoon. Serve with parsley garnish.

Tomato Pepper Pasta

3 sweet Red Peppers
4 red Potatoes
4 large ripe Tomatoes
1/4 c black Olives, pitted
1/4 c sun-dried Tomatoes, sliced
1/4 c fresh Basil, chopped
1 lb Pasta noodles
1 small head Radicchio, shredded

Halve the peppers, remove seeds and membranes. Place in single layer on baking sheet, skin side up. Broil until slightly blackened. Let cool, peel and cut into chunks.

Cook potatoes until tender. Let cool, cut into chunks. Core tomatoes, cut into chunks. Combine tomatoes, peppers, potatoes, olives, sun-dried tomatoes and basil in large mixing bowl.

Dressing:
1/2 c Olive Oil
2 tbsp red wine Vinegar
1 clove Garlic, minced
1 tsp Anchovy paste
1/2 tsp Salt
1/4 tsp hot Pepper flakes
1/4 tsp fresh ground Pepper

Whisk together oil, vinegar, garlic, anchovy paste, salt, pepper flakes and pepper. Pour over tomato mixture.

Cook pasta until tender. Drain well, toss immediately with tomato mixture. Serve warm on bed of shredded radicchio, with a Gewurtraminer wine.

(Did you know that tomatoes were thought to be poisonous until Ben Franklin ate one to disprove the theory? I presume that while flying the kite in the thunderstorm, he had forgotten to pack a lunch, reached down for the nearest edible, and zap!)

Classico Tomato Salad

4 ripe Tomatoes
1 can Artichoke hearts
1 c Mozzarella cheese, cubed
1/2 sweet green Pepper, diced
1 green Onion, chopped
1/2 c fresh Basil, chopped coarsely
1/3 c black Olives, chopped
1/3 c Lemon juice
Salt and fresh ground Pepper to taste

Core tomatoes, chop into chunks. Drain artichokes, quarter. Combine tomatoes, artichoke hearts, mozzarella, peppers, basil, olives and onion. Drizzle with oil and lemon juice and toss. Season with salt and pepper to taste. Serve with chilled white Zinfandel wine.

Quilt Inn Country Cookbook

Oriental Tomato Salad

3 large ripe Tomatoes
1 Cucumber
1/2 c fresh Parsley, chopped
1/2 c fresh Mint, chopped
1/2 c fresh Coriander, chopped
3 green Onions, chopped
1 Spanish Onion, sliced thin

Core tomatoes, cut into slices. Score cucumber lengthwise with fork, slice thinly. Combine parsley, coriander, mint and onions.

In serving bowl, layer Spanish onions, cucumber, and tomatoes, sprinkling parsley mixture between layers.

Dressing:
3 tbsp Lemon juice
2 tbsp Soya sauce
1 tbsp Sugar
1/4 tsp Salt
1/3 c Vegetable Oil
2 cloves Garlic, minced
Dash hot Pepper flakes

Whisk together lemon juice, soya sauce, sugar and salt until sugar is dissolved. Whisk in oil, garlic and pepper flakes. Pour over salad, set aside for 30 minutes at room temperature to marinate. Chill before serving.

Stuffed Tomatoes

Preheat oven to 400F and lightly grease a baking sheet.

Slice off top quarter of six large meaty tomatoes. Scoop out insides being careful not to cut through to skin. Save scrapings from 3 tomatoes in mixing bowl. Turn tomatoes upside down on paper towels to drain.

Stuffing:
1 lb fresh Spinach, washed and chopped
6 slices Bacon, chopped into pieces
1 c fresh Mushrooms, sliced
3 green Onions, chopped fine
3 tbsp dry Breadcrumbs
1/2 tsp Salt
Fresh ground Pepper to taste
6 tsp Butter

Cook bacon until crisp in small skillet. Remove from skillet and place on paper towels to drain. Pour excess fat from skillet, leaving enough to saute green onions and mushrooms until golden brown. Using slotted spoon, remove from pan and add to tomato pulp in mixing bowl.

Steam spinach until it is wilted. Drain and press out as much moisture as possible. Chop coarsely and add to tomato pulp mixture. Stir 2 tablespoons of breadcrumbs into mixture. Toss lightly with salt and pepper.

Pat dry the insides of the tomato shells. Spoon spinach mixture into each tomato and sprinkle with remaining breadcrumbs. Top each with teaspoon of butter.

Place tomatoes on baking sheet with tops. Bake for 25 minutes or until tomatoes are cooked but still firm. Replace tomato tops before serving.

For an Alternative Stuffing, to the tomato pulp add:

1 1/2 c whole corn kernels (frozen will do)
1/3 c green onions, chopped fine
1/3 c sweet green Pepper, chopped fine
4 tbsp fresh Basil, chopped
1 Jalapeno Pepper, seeded and chopped fine
2 tbsp fresh Coriander, chopped
1/2 c sharp old Cheese, crumbled
1/2 tsp Salt
Fresh ground Pepper to taste

Toss all ingredients together lightly until well mixed. Fill tomato shells. Sprinkle each tomato with yellow Cornmeal and dot with butter. Bake as above.

Umberto's Famous Pasta Sauce

4 large ripe Plum Tomatoes
3 tbsp Butter, unsalted
2 cloves Garlic, minced
1/3 c Chicken stock
1/4 c dry white Wine
4 tsp fresh Basil, chopped fine
1/2 tsp Salt
1/4 fresh ground Pepper

Peel, seed and chop tomatoes. Melt 1 tbsp butter over medium heat, cook garlic until soft. Pour in stock and wine, simmer uncovered 3 to 5 minutes or until reduced by half. Add tomatoes, basil and remaining butter. Cook for 2 to 3 minutes, stirring constantly, until flavours are blended. Add salt and pepper. Serve tossed over angel's hair pasta, garnish with Parmesan cheese. Serve with red Merlot wine.

Chili Sauce

14 c ripe Tomatoes, peeled and chopped
4 c peeled Cucumber, chopped
3 c Onions, chopped
2 tbsp Pickling Spice
3 c Sugar
2 c cider Vinegar
2 tsp Celery seed
1/2 tsp Turmeric
1/2 tsp Curry powder
2 tbsp all-purpose Flour
4 c Water

Boil water and combine with cucumbers, onions and salt. Let stand 1 hour.

Mix Tomatoes, sugar, 1 cup of vinegar, celery seed, turmeric and curry powder in saucepan. Bring to boil, stirring often. Reduce heat, simmer for 30 minutes while stirring.

Drain cucumber mixture, rinse well with cold water and drain. Add tomato mixture. Simmer for 2 hours or until vegetables are tender and mixture reduces to 11 cups.

Combine flour with remaining vinegar, stir into sauce. Cook 5 to 10 minutes longer bringing to boil and thickening. Pour into sterilized jars. Cover with new lids and seal.

The famous french chef, Brillat-Savarin, once said, "Poultry is for the cook what the canvas is for the painter." That may be true, but have you ever tried to paint a chicken?

Bonnie Stern's Chicken and Tomato Fondue

6 Chicken breasts
1/3 c Olive Oil
3 tbsp Lime juice
1 tbsp fresh Rosemary
1/2 tsp fresh ground Pepper

Remove skin and fat from chicken. Place in shallow glass dish. Combine oil, lime juice, rosemary and pepper, pour over chicken. Cover and marinate for 30 minutes at room temperature or overnight in refrigerator.

Drain chicken and pat dry. Broil or barbecue until chicken is no longer pink inside, basting with marinade.

Serve chicken with tomato fondue, garnish with parsley. Serve with white Chardonnay wine.

Tomato Fondue:
5 ripe Tomatoes
6 cloves Garlic unpeeled
4 Anchovy fillets, chopped fine
1 tbsp fresh Thyme
Dash hot Pepper flakes
2 tbsp Olive Oil
Salt and fresh ground Pepper to taste

Place tomatoes and garlic in shallow glass baking dish. Scatter anchovies, thyme, pepper flakes on top. Drizzle with olive oil. Bake in 400F over for 40 to 45 minutes or until tomatoes are soft and garlic is tender. Let cool. Peel halve and seed tomatoes. Peel garlic.

Puree tomatoes and garlic until smooth. Transfer puree to saucepan. Cook over medium heat, stirring often, for 15 minutes or until thickened and reduced by one-third. Season with salt and pepper to taste. Serve over chicken.

Classic Thick Tomato Sauce

1/4 c Olive Oil
1 large Onion, chopped
1 c Celery, diced
10 lb Plum Tomatoes, peeled
2 Potatoes
2 Carrots, peeled
1 tsp Salt
1 tsp dried Oregano
2 large sprigs fresh Basil
2 large sprigs fresh Parsley
1/4 tsp fresh ground Pepper

Heat oil over medium heat in large saucepan, cook onion and celery until soft (about 6 minutes). In blender, finely chop tomatoes in batches. Add tomatoes, potatoes, carrots, salt, oregano, basil and parsley to saucepan. Bring to boil, stirring frequently. Reduce heat and simmer, uncovered, for 3 hours or until reduced by one-third and sauce is thick.

Remove herb sprigs and discard. Remove potatoes and carrots, mash and return to sauce to add thickening.

Tomato Bruschetta

15 ripe Plum tomatoes
2/3 c extra virgin Olive oil
1 c fresh Basil leaves, chopped
6 cloves Garlic, minced
6 cloves Garlic, slivered
1/4 c green Onions, chopped fine
1 tsp Lemon juice
Salt and fresh ground Pepper to taste

Thick cut coarse bread.

Chop tomatoes and toss in bowl with garlic and green onions and basil. Add lemon juice, salt and pepper and 1/3 c olive oil.

Saute slivered garlic in 1/3 c olive oil until golden brown. Discard garlic and reserve oil.

Toast bread and brush with garlic-flavored oil. Spoon tomato mixture over bread, and serve.

Hunka Hunka Burnin' Love

We had a special guest drop by the other day. Bill Parker was passing through town, and, needing a place to stay, was recommended to The Quilt Inn by Horace the pump jockey down at the Service Station across from the Cheese Shoppe.

We're always delighted to learn new and interesting things from our visitors, but Bill's comments, on sitting down to one of our home-cooked meals, took us back a bit.

"Not very spicy," he said, adding more pepper from the pepper mill. "Do you have any Tabasco Sauce, or better yet, Sauce from Hell?" The latter, I learned, is a local specialty in his town Bill was quite well acquainted with. It's prime ingredient is chilis, and of course this led to a conversation about these fiery little devils.

Bill travels out of his native state a lot and was well prepared for the relatively bland tastebuds of "foreigners"; he had some habanero peppers in his carry bag which he generously offered to share with me. One taste, and the heat was so intense I nearly fainted. With a gasp I asked Michael for three things: water, dial "911", and last rites.

Most people would avoid such incendiary peppers. Not Bill and his asbestos-lined fellow gastronomes. They crave the heat.

Once I had recovered, Bill explained that a true pepper fiend wouldn't even flinch at the ordinary jalapeno, considering it child's play.

"Myself, I particularly like the scotch bonnet," said Bill, a native of Louisiana where his mother had introduced him to the taste of spicy food. I'm rather fond of an occasional drink, and the image of a "scotch bonnet" produced a vision of Bushmill's neat in a glass with a paper hat on it. It turns out that the scotch bonnet is a close cousin to the habanero, related in the same way as the Hatfields and the McCoys, who incidentally at this very time were having a war of their own in my stomach. These two peppers are kings of the Scoville Scale, a system that rates peppers based on capsaicin content, the compound that makes chilis hot.

At the bottom of the Scoville is the green bell pepper, with 0 Scoville Heat Units, or "H.U." The jalapeno, Bill said, comes in around 2,500 to 5,000 H.U.'s. The habanero and scotch bonnet fall into the 100,000 to 300,000 H.U. range. Other hot chilis include the Thai, at 50,000 to 100,000 H.U., and the pequin, cayenne, and Tabasco peppers at 30,000 to 50,000 H.U., and the arbol, 15,000 to 30,000 H.U.

So, if you want to take the chili plunge, what do you do with them? Here's what Bill suggests: chilis will grow mold in a few short days. Store them in a dry place for up to a week, or preserve them by roasting. A warning: handle the exotic chilis with care. Some can blister the skin, so wear rubber gloves, and do not touch your eyes with hands still contaminated.

Roast Chilis If You Dare

Cut a small slit in the chili close to the end to let the steam escape. Place the chili on a baking sheet directly under the broiler and turn with tongs. Or, bake them in a 375F oven for 30 minutes. When the chili darkens and blisters, remove from heat and place in a plastic bag or damp paper towels for 10 or 15 minutes. Remove from bag and peel away skin. Chilis can be frozen in freezer bags for convenient use.

When do you use chilis, and where? "Anytime, anyplace," Bill informed us. "Anything you make or eat can be spiced up with a liberal, or conservative, sprinkling of fresh or roasted chilis."

And with that, Bill drove away, leaving us to ponder this new information, and whether or not our guests could handle the heat. But as my Grama would say, "If you can't handle the heat, stay out of the kitchen!" Or was that someone else. No mind.

✳ ✳ ✳

Pasta Peppers Please

1 sweet red Pepper, roasted, peeled and seeded
1 clove Garlic, chopped
1/2 c grated Parmesan Cheese
1 tbsp ground Almonds
1 tbsp Olive Oil
1 tbsp Cream Cheese
Dash hot pepper sauce
Salt and pepper to taste
1/2 lb cooked Pasta
fresh Basil

In blender or food processor, puree garlic. Blend in red pepper, half the cheese, the almonds, oils, cream cheese and hot pepper sauce. Season with salt and pepper. Toss with pasta. Sprinkle with remaining Parmesan cheese. Garnish with basil and serve with white Zinfandel wine.

Harvest Vegetables with Chili

2 tbsp Vegetable Oil
1 large red Onion, chopped
2 cloves Garlic, minced
2 Zucchini, cubed
2 sweet red or yellow Peppers, cubed
1 large Eggplant, cubed
1 tbsp chopped hot Pepper
4 tsp Chili powder
1 tsp Cumin
1 tsp Salt
1 tsp Oregano
3 c chopped Tomatoes
2 1/2 c water or Chicken Stock
1 1/2 c green Lentils
2 tbsp Lemon juice

In large saucepan heat oil over medium heat. Cook onion and garlic, stirring occasionally, for 4 minutes or until soft. Add zucchini, sweet peppers, eggplant and hot pepper. Cook, stirring, for 5 minutes. Stir in chili powder, cumin, salt, oregano. Cook for 5 minutes. Add tomatoes, water, and lentils. Bring to boil. Reduce to low heat and cook for 40 to 45 minutes or until lentils are tender. For thicker chili, uncover and cook to desired consistency. Stir in lemon juice and salt to taste. Serve with crusty bread or cornbread.

From the Believe it or not file: A Carolina paint company is producing a line of marine paints from Bill's beloved jalapeno peppers that keeps barnacles off boat bottoms without polluting harbors. If barnacles won't touch the stuff... And, apparently they're working with the even hotter Habaneros. I'm glad to see a non-chemical environmental answer to the barnacle problem. Now if you told me they were making a paint remover from the incendiary little devils I would believe it!

Fresh Salsa

1 1/2 c diced seeded and peeled Tomatoes
1/4 c chopped red Onion
1/4 c chopped sweet yellow Pepper
2 tbsp chopped Celery
2 tbsp Olive Oil
1 tbsp red wine or cider vinegar
1 1/2 tsp fresh hot Pepper
1/4 c chopped Parsley

Combine tomatoes, onion, yellow pepper, celery, oil, vinegar and hot pepper. Cover and let stand for 20 minutes for flavors to blend. Stir in parsley. Season with salt and pepper to taste and more hot pepper if desired. Serve as condiment on hamburgers, with grilled chicken, tacos or omelettes.

Cooked Salsa

4 c chopped peeled Tomatoes
1 c chopped sweet red Peppers
1 c chopped sweet green Peppers
1 c hot Peppers
1 c chopped Onion
1/3 c Sugar
1 clove Garlic, minced
1 tsp Salt
1 1/2 c cider Vinegar

In large saucepan, combine tomatoes, sweet peppers, hot peppers, onion, sugar, garlic and salt; pour in vinegar. Bring to boil and reduce to low heat. Cook, stirring occasionally, for 45 minutes or until thickened slightly. Let cool. Refrigerate up to one month. Serve as condiment.

Salsa and Cheese

2 c medium Cheddar cheese, grated
8 oz Cream cheese
1 tbsp Dijon mustard
1/2 tsp hot Pepper sauce
1 c crushed Nachos

Preheat oven to 400F and grease baking sheet.

Cream together Cheddar and cream cheese, mustard, pepper and hot pepper sauce. Shape into 1/2 inch thick rounds (8 to 10). Press into nacho crumbs until well coated. Place on greased baking sheet. Set aside. (May be made ahead and refrigerated.)

Salsa:
6 ripe Tomatoes
1/2 c fresh Parsley, chopped
1/2 c fresh Coriander, chopped
4 green Onions, chopped
2 Jalapeno Peppers, seeded and chopped
2 cloves Garlic, minced
1/2 tsp Salt

Core, seed and dice tomatoes, drain well in sieve. Combine tomatoes, parsley, coriander, onions, peppers, garlic and salt. Transfer mixture to serving bowl or individual plates with slotted spoon.

Before serving, bake cheese rounds for 3 to 5 minutes or until cheese is warm but not too runny. Remove from baking sheet with spatula and serve on top of salsa. Serve with crusty bread and Sauvignon Blanc wine.

Creamy Salsa Dip

1 c Tomatoes, seeded and chopped
1/4 c Onion, chopped
1 clove Garlic, crushed
1 tsp Chili powder
1 c Cream cheese
2 tbsp Mayonnaise
Dash Salt
Fresh ground Pepper to taste

Blend cream cheese and mayonnaise. Stir in remaining ingredients. Cover and chill. Serve with crudites (those are badly behaved vegetables) and nachos.

Hot and Sweet Pepper Relish

4 c prepared Sweet Peppers (3 green, 3 red and 5 jalapeno)
3/4 c Apple cider vinegar
3 1/4 c Sugar
1 box Certo Fruit Pectin Crystals

Halve peppers, discard seeds, chop fine. Measure 4 cups including juice, into saucepan. Add vinegar. Mix fruit pectin crystals with 1/4 cup sugar. Blend well.

Slowly add pectin mixture to peppers in saucepan. Cook over high heat, stirring constantly until mixture comes to boil. Stir in remaining sugar. Return to boil while stirring and boil for 1 minute.

Remove from heat. Skim off foam with spoon. Pour into sterilized jars, cover with new lids or paraffin wax. Store opened relish in refrigerator.

Green Chili Stew With Pork

Jeff Smith, the Frugal Gourmet, devised this firebrand recipe.

3 lb boneless Pork, cubed
3 tbsp Peanut Oil
3 stalks Celery, chopped
2 medium Tomatoes, diced
7 green Chilis, roasted, peeled and chopped
4 cloves Garlic, crushed
Chicken stock
Salt to taste
La Victoria Salsa Jalapeno

Brown pork in oil in small batches. Place seared meat in large ovenproof (fireproof!) casserole. Add celery, tomatoes, chilis and garlic. Deglaze frying pan with chicken stock and add to pot. Cover ingredients with stock to cover. Cover and simmer until stew is thick and the meat is tender, about 1 1/2 hours. Add salt to taste.

Add a bit of La Victoria salsa jalapeno for more heat, if you dare. Serve with potatoes, or cornbread.

Chili Slaw for the Brave

1 each sweet red, green, orange and yellow Pepper
1 red Onion

Core, seed and slice all peppers in salad bowl. Peel and cut onion into slices, separate rings. Toss together and set aside.

Dressing:
1 Jalapeno pepper, cored, seeded and minced
2 tbsp tarragon Vinegar
1 tbsp Dijon mustard
2 tsp Sugar
1/4 c Olive oil
2 tbsp Sesame oil
1/4 tsp Hot sauce *(Tabasco will do)*
1 tbsp Caraway seeds, toasted
3 tsp Lemon or Lime zest, grated

Combine all ingredients, except oils, zest and caraway seeds, in mixing bowl. Slowly pour in oils while whisking briskly, until dressing is smooth and thick. Toss with peppers. Sprinkle with caraway seeds and zest until well coated. Cover and chill for 2 hours before serving.

Who Will Pick Up My Stitches When I'm Gone?

We went to a funeral today. A woman in the Quilt Guild passed away from cancer. She left a grief-stricken husband and bereft teenage daughter. She had been an active quilter for many years and an important member of the guild.

Her death was so sudden it caught everyone by surprise, including her, I think. Her last quilt was still in the frame in a corner of the living room. Where the quilt extended past the area held by the frame, there were many lengths of thread hanging loose, ready to be re-threaded and continued on along the pencilled quilt lines. I was filled with eerie tingles as I looked at the unfinished quilt. Surely Carol would return any minute now and sit down at the frame.

Carol's daughter had left the frame standing, and as the guild members came by the house, she welcomed them in, and softly asked each of us if we would put a few stitches in her Mom's last quilt. Each of us in turn picked up Carol's needles and thread, and carefully matched our stitches to hers. It felt somehow like an intrusion into someone else's work, and at the same time, felt like a connection, a final communion, with Carol.

Carol's daughter, a modern teenager, had never bothered to learn to quilt. She didn't need to; her mother would make her anything she wanted. Today, however, she asked us to show her how and she sat with us for a long time struggling with the unfamiliar stitching technique. She is determined now to finish her mother's quilt. The members offered to help. We are going to take over a full size quilt frame next week and put Carol's quilt in it. That will allow several women to sit and quilt at the same time, instead of just one. Quilting should be a communal activity.

Every Tuesday evening, whoever is available will go over and quilt with Carol's daughter. There is a teenage daughter who needs to find her mother, and we, her mother's friends, will sit by her as she does so.

When I think about picking up the stitches that Carol left

unsewn, I wonder who will pick up my own unfinished stitches when I'm gone.

* * *

Hostess Dishes

It's a tradition in most country communities that a wake follows a funeral. Because the grief-sticken family is usually in no state of mind or preparation to "entertain" large numbers of guests, it's also tradition that everyone brings one of their own family dishes for the guests at the wake, and for the family to use in the days thereafter until life goes back to a semblance of being normal.

These easy-to-prepare hostess dishes are just as handy for happier occasions -- "welcome to the neighborhood" get-togethers, "congratulations on the new baby" events, or just pot luck suppers -- whenever families and friends get together to share food and love. These dishes can often be made at a moment's notice from whatever is in the refrigerator and are also good "second-day" meals, using left-overs from the dinner the day before, making them economical. Don't be afraid to substitute ingredients -- these recipes are not written in stone!

Turkey Tracks Casserole

2 c cooked Turkey
1/2 lb fresh Mushrooms
1/4 c Onion, chopped
1 c wild Rice
1 1/2 c Cream
2 1/2 c turkey Stock (chicken will do)
1/2 c Cheddar cheese, grated
Salt and fresh ground Pepper to taste

Quilt Inn Country Cookbook

Preheat oven to 350F

Wash wild rice in water several times to remove starch and soak in cold water for 1 hour. Drain rice and place in mixing bowl with turkey, mushrooms, cream, onion, salt and pepper. Mix well. Add stock and pour into ovenproof casserole. Bake for 1 1/2 hours. Sprinkle with grated cheese and bake additional 20 minutes until cheese melts.

Carol's ABC Casserole

A - 2 lb fresh Asparagus (frozen will do)
B - 6 strips Bacon, cooked crisp and chopped
C - 1 lb cooked Chicken
2 cans condensed Mushroom soup
1/2 c Cream
1/4 tsp Curry powder
Dash hot sauce
1/4 c Pimientos, chopped
1/4 c Parmesan cheese, grated

Preheat oven to 400F

Layer asparagus, chicken and bacon crumbles in lightly greased casserole dish. Mix soup, cream, curry powder, hot sauce and pimientos in saucepan and cook on medium heat, stirring, until blended and smooth. Pour over chicken mixture. Sprinkle with Parmesan cheese. Bake for 20 minutes or until heated thoroughly. Place under broiler to brown cheese.

Aliske Webb

Shrimp Casserole

1/2 lb Shrimp, cleaned and deveined
1/4 c green Pepper, chopped
1/4 c Onion, chopped
2 c cooked wild Rice
2 tbsp Butter
1 can condensed Mushroom soup
1/2 tsp dry Mustard
1/2 tsp Worcestershire sauce
1/2 c Cheddar cheese, cubed

Preheat oven to 375F

Saute onion and green pepper in butter. Add wild rice, mushroom soup, mustard powder, Worcestershire sauce, shrimp and cheese. Pour into casserole and bake for 30 to 40 minutes.

Almondine Rice

2 c wild Rice
3/4 c Almonds, chopped lengthwise
1/2 c Olive oil
1/4 c Onion, chopped
1/4 c Chives, chopped
1/4 c green Onions, chopped
1/4 c green Pepper, chopped
4 1/2 c (chicken) Stock
Salt and fresh ground Pepper to taste

Preheat oven to 325 F

Wash rice several times to remove starch. Soak in cold water for 1 hour. Drain rice.

Saute onion, chives, green onion and green pepper until tender. Add rice and cook, while stirring, over low heat until rice begins to turn clear. Add stock and salt and pepper. Mix in almonds. Bake for 1 1/2 hours or until rice is cooked and liquid is absorbed.

Broccoli and Cauliflower Casserole

1 1/2 c Broccoli florets, steamed but still crisp
1 1/2 c Cauliflower florets, steamed but still crisp
1/4 c Butter
1/4 c all-purpose Flour
2 1/2 c Milk
1 tsp Curry powder
1 tbsp Apricot chutney or jam
Salt and fresh ground Pepper to taste
1 c Swiss cheese, grated

Preheat oven to 350F

Melt butter in saucepan. Whisk in flour. Cook 2-3 minutes, stirring, but do not brown.

Whisk in milk. Bring to a full boil. Stir in curry and chutney. Reduce heat. Simmer for 5 minutes. Add salt and pepper. Stir in cheese. Cook until cheese melts.

Place broccoli and cauliflower in buttered casserole. Pour sauce over top.

Topping:
1/4 c melted Butter
1 1/2 c Breadcrumbs
1/2 c sliced Almonds, toasted

Mix all ingredients together and sprinkle over vegetables and sauce. Bake for 20 minutes or until bubbling.

Waldorf Pasta Casserole

1 1/2 c elbow Macaroni, cooked
1 lb Spinach, steamed and chopped
2 c Bean sprouts
1 lb Feta cheese
2 Onions, chopped and sauteed

1/2 c Walnuts, chopped
2 Eggs
1/3 c Milk
Fresh ground Pepper to taste

Preheat oven to 350F and lightly grease casserole.

Combine macaroni, spinach, sprouts, cheese, walnuts and onion in lightly greased ovenproof dish. Beat egg and milk together and pour over casserole. Sprinkle with pepper. Bake for 20 minutes or until bubbly.

Pork and Potato Casserole

1 pork tenderloin, cut into medallions
3 c Potatoes, sliced thin
1 c Onion, sliced thin
1 clove Garlic, minced
4 tbsp Dijon mustard
2 tsp dried Thyme
2 c heavy Cream
1/4 c dry white Wine
Fresh ground Pepper to taste

Preheat oven to 350F.

In a saucepan, bring cream and garlic to boil. Reduce heat and simmer 6-8 minutes or until reduced by one third. Add mustard, thyme and mix well. Set aside.

Steam potatoes for 30 seconds so potatoes are still crisp. Drain and rinse in cold water. Pat dry on paper towels. Brown pork medallions in skillet over medium-high heat. Remove chops and set aside. Use wine to deglaze skillet.

In ovenproof casserole dish, layer half the potatoes and onions; lay pork on top and pour pan juices over. Top with remaining potatoes and onions. Pour reduced cream over top. Sprinkle with pepper. Bake for 1 1/2 hours.

The Wrong Arm of the Law

Early this morning Jeff Bob Burnet, the town sheriff, dropped by to return our post-hole digger. We sat for a spell in rocking chairs on the verandah. There are strings that run from the garden to the carved wood "gingerbread" trim that runs under the verandah eaves where morning glories and string beans grow up. It makes a nice dappled shade on the verandah in the morning as it just starts to get too hot.

As we enjoyed a morning coffee, we shared some local gossip and I was reminded of the story about how Jeff Bob got to be sherrif. Jeff Bob's always been something of a loose cannon as a sheriff but you would have a hard time replacing him now. His notoriety and popularity came as a result of his unbridled and perhaps unwise enthusiasm in running for the job of sheriff.

County elections are usually low key and uninteresting events around here, and in most other places for that matter. There's the usual flutter of handmade support signs that litter lawns and shop windows for several weeks.

The local newspaper carries each nominee's election ad, which is usually not much more than conservative resumes and raison de vote. The strength of most nominees' credentials seems to lie on their stable homelife (wife, 3 kids, dog Spot) and number of years in the community. Knowledge of law is never much of a factor. Not much remarkable happens, and then the keys to the two-cell jail building change hands quietly. And life goes on.

Until the year Jeff Bob decided to run. Which is tough to do when you have your foot in your mouth. Jeff Bob was decidedly at a disadvantage since he's a forty-plus bachelor and only moved here five years previously after being laid off from a steelworker's job. He came, temporarily, to help his brother-in-law, and ended up staying. It often happens that way.

But Jeff Bob brought some personal dark clouds with him. It seems there was a great deal of rancor and hard feelings at the steel plant between the management and workers. He was one of the many caught in a political and financial crossfire and he deeply resented the unpredictable outcome, "out you go". I guess he was still stinging from the surprise, and earnestly felt it was such an important issue, and, since he had no sterling family and background to tout, that he unwisely reassured the townsfolk in his brief campaign ad that if elected he would always maintain an "open door policy" with regards to his job as sheriff. He meant there would be no surprises.

It was a deadly phrase. The small ad never did explain his intention behind the phrase. Brevity lead to levity. What sort of town has an open door jail?

The morning the newspaper hit the sidewalk there was mixed hilarity and consternation around town. He meant, of course, open door to the community, not to offenders, but that's not how it sounded and the local wags razzed him mercilessly for weeks before the election. It was hard to tell if the red face JB stomped around town in was from embarrassment, or anger.

The surprise came on election day, and none was more surprised than Jeff Bob when he won. Perhaps the wags felt they owed him their vote, to give him back his face. Perhaps there were enough people around town, like myself, who think you just gotta vote for a guy with either the silliness or the earnestness to profess an open door policy for a jail.

So now it's passed into being a gentle joke. Even Jeff Bob wears it lightly. Although we're still a town divided. There are those who want to put up a sign proclaiming our status as a town with an open door policy jail, and those who are definitely not amused at all.

* * *

Jeff Bob's Open Door Butter Tarts

Preheat oven to 425F, grease 12 muffin or tart pans.

1 Pastry double-piecrust
1/2 c packed Brown Sugar
1/2 c Corn Syrup
1/4 c Shortening
1 Egg, lightly beaten
1 tsp Vanilla
1/4 tsp Salt
3/4 c Raisins

Roll out piecrust on floured surface. Cut into 4 inch rounds. Fit into tart pans. Combine all ingredients, mixing well. Sprinkle raisins in pastry shells. Fill each shell 2/3 full with syrup mixture. Bake on bottom of oven for 12-15 minutes or until set. Don't overbake them. Cool on wire rack, then remove from pans.

Break Out Chocolate Chip Cookies

1/2 c Butter
1/2 c Shortening
1 c Sugar
1/2 Brown Sugar
2 tsp Vanilla
2 Eggs
2 c all-purpose Flour
1 tsp Baking Soda
2 c Chocolate Chips

Preheat oven to 350F, grease cookie sheets. Cream together butter and shortening. Gradually add sugars, creaming well. Beat in eggs and vanilla. In separate bowl, combine flour and baking soda. Blend into cream mixture. Stir in chocolate chips. Chill dough for several minutes.

Drop by spoonsfuls onto greased baking sheets. Flatten slightly.

Aliske Webb

(If you drop high enough, no need to flatten!) Bake for 8 to 9 minutes or until golden brown around edges. Let cool on sheet before removing. Set on wire racks to finish cooling.

Sweet 'N Sour Key Lime Pie Worth Stealing

Serve in small, small pieces. You might look cheap -- until people taste how rich this is!

Crust:
1 c Graham cracker crumbs
1 1/2 tsp icing sugar
1/2 tsp Cinnamon
5 tbsp melted Butter

Combine crumbs, icing sugar and cinnamon in 9-inch pie plate. Pour in butter and blend well. Pat mixture firmly to form crust. Chill 30 minutes or until firm.

Preheat oven to 350F.

Filling:
3 Egg yolks
1 can sweetened Condensed Milk
Rind of 1 lime, finely grated
1/2 c fresh lime juice (about 3 limes)

Beat egg yolks. Slowly beat in milk, mixing well. Stir in rind and juice. Pour into prepared shell. Bake for 12 minutes or until barely set. Remove and cool. Serve at room temperature for the best flavour. Garnish with whip cream and thinly sliced fresh lime if desired.

Quilt Inn Country Cookbook

Aunt Ivy's Three Fruit Cobbler

8 c mixed fruit - peach, plums, apricots - chopped
1/2 c sugar
1 1/2 tsp all-purpose Flour
Zest of 1 Orange
1 tsp Cinnamon

Preheat oven to 400F, and lightly grease 12-inch square glass baking dish.

Cut fruit into chunks, mix with sugar, flour, cinnamon and zest. Spoon into baking dish.

Topping:
1 1/2 c all-purpose Flour
1 tsp Baking powder
1/2 tsp Baking soda
1/4 tsp Salt
1/2 c Sugar
6 tbsp cold Butter
2 Eggs
1 c buttermilk
1 tsp Vanilla extract
2 drops Almond extract
1/4 c blanched Almonds, sliced

Sift dry ingredients together. Cut in butter with pastry cutter or two kitchen knives until coarse lumps are formed. Blend in eggs, buttermilk, vanilla and almond extracts. Spoon over fruit and spread evenly. Sprinkle with almonds. Bake for 30 minutes or until golden brown and firm to the touch. Cool on wire rack. Serve warm or chilled.

Date, Nut and Oatmeal Loaf

1/2 c Flour
1 tsp baking Soda
1 tsp Cinnamon

1 tsp Cloves
3/4 c Butter
2 c dark brown Sugar
2 Eggs
1 1/2 c Dates, chopped fine
1 c Walnuts, chopped coarsely
2 c rolled Oats

Preheat oven to 350F and grease loaf pan.

Sift flour, soda, cinnamon and cloves together in a mixing bowl. Pour 1 cup boiling water over rolled oats, mix well. Cool, then blend in butter, sugar, eggs, dates and walnuts. Blend into dry ingredients and mix well. Bake for 45 to 55 minutes or until done.

Jailhouse Molasses Bars

1/3 c Margarine or Shortening
1 c white Sugar
1 Egg, well beaten
1/2 c Molasses
1 tsp Baking soda
2 tsp hot Water
2 1/2 c cake and pastry Flour
1/2 tsp Cinnamon
1/2 tsp Ginger

Preheat oven to 350F

Cream margarine and sugar. Add egg and molasses. Dissolve baking soda in hot water and add to mixture. Add dry ingredients. Batter should be quite stiff. Smooth into baking pan. Dust top with granulated sugar and pat with fingers. Bake 35 minutes or until done.

Pumpkin Cookies

These make a nice change from your standard chocolate chip or oatmeal cookies.

1/2 c Margarine
2 Eggs
2 to 2 1/2 c Flour
1 c rolled Oats
1 tsp Cinnamon
1/2 tsp Nutmeg
3/4 c brown Sugar
3/4 c Pumpkin pie filling
1/3 c Raisins
3 tsp Baking powder
Dash salt

Preheat oven to 350F and grease baking sheets.

Sift dry ingredients together in mixing bowl. Gradually blend in margarine, eggs and pumpkin. Drop by teaspoons onto baking sheet. Bake 20 minutes or until done.

Gingersnaps

4 1/2 c all-purpose Flour
2 1/2 c dark brown Sugar
2 c Butter, softened
3 Eggs
3/4 c Molasses
1/4 c ground Ginger
1 1/2 tsp ground Cinnamon
1 1/2 tsp Baking soda
1/2 tsp Salt

Preheat oven to 325F and grease baking sheets.

Cream butter and sugar in large mixing bowl until light and fluffy. Beat in eggs and then molasses.

Sift together flour, ginger, cinnamon, soda and salt. Stir dry ingredients into butter mixture until thoroughly mixed. Cover for 30 minutes and set aside.

Drop batter by spoonfuls onto baking sheets. Flatten cookies. Bake for 10 to 15 minutes or until browned. Let cookies cool slightly then place on wire racks to cool.

"Uncle Al" Brown's Apple Pie

9 inch pastry shell, unbaked

5 c Apples, peeled, cored and sliced
2/3 c Sugar
1 tbsp Cornstarch
1/2 tsp Cinnamon
1/8 tsp Cloves
1/8 tsp Allspice
3 tbsp Butter, softened
1 c Cheddar cheese, grated

Preheat oven to 425F and line pie plate with pastry.

In large mixing bowl pour melted butter over apples and toss gently, coating apples thoroughly.

In small mixing bowl combine sugar, cornstarch and spices. Sprinkle 1 tablespoon of this mixture over pieshell. Add remaining spice mixture to apples, tossing gently.

Spoon apples into pieshell and bake for 30 minutes or until apples are tender. Remove from oven and sprinkle cheese over apples. Return to oven for 3 minutes or until cheese melts. Serve warm.

Send The Servants to the Cellar

If you rise early enough you may see a dusty old pickup truck parked in our yard. It belongs to one of the many invisible people who help make an Inn run smoothly: Clareville's only resident Russian emigree, Tamara Shostokovitch. *("Not* that *one, darling, he was* much *too bourgeois.")* Tamara is anywhere upwards of seventy -- it's your guess. And although she wears grubby old American blue jeans, her frazzled grey hair is still held back by a colorful *Babushka*, the ubiquitous large Russian kerchief.

Tamara runs a small market garden and supplies us with fresh vegetables such as potatoes, cabbage and squash, common vegetables to be sure, but staples that are familiar and comfortable to her because they recall her childhood in a very different Russia than today. She even delivers to us once a fortnight because she comes from "the old school" when a fortnight meant something. What it means is, we *never* know when she's coming. She's always welcome.

This morning, after we helped her unload her produce into the root cellar, we all went to the kitchen for a cup of coffee because today Tamara brought with her a treasure from her homeland to share with us: a copy of *A Gift to Young Housewives* by Elena Molokhovets. This wonderful book was a serious work at the time, but now is both hilarious and nostalgic, and I'd like to share some of it with you.

The *Gift* first appeared in Russia in 1861, the year of the emancipation of the serfs ("serfs up!" was therefore introduced into the local lexicon). This huge volume of over 4,200 recipes provides us with a window from which to view a lost and somewhat forgotten age, where a well-run household, serfless (see poor humor above) yet with servants, was equal only to running a major corporation today. The young Russian bride needed all the organizational capabilities of a major-general.

In fact, the author, Elena Molokhovets, was from a military family, and her meal preparations came by her honestly: she had ten children, nine boys and a girl, as well as many grandchildren, either too numerous to count or missing from the Russian census. The *Gift* was an instant and utter success, and Elena continued to revise, edit (although clearly with a light hand) and add to the book for another 50 years, when she disappeared without a trace, presumably a victim of the Revolution, or indigestion.

After the Revolution, she was quoted widely, albeit sarcastically, in Soviet circles, such as her answer to the problem of unexpected guests: "Send the servant into the cold cellar for hazel grouse or a ham." Many of Lenin's followers held her responsible for representing the excesses of bygone days. Is Julia Child's fate to be the same?

Anyway, after a few years, the acerbic humor became more wistful -- remembrances of the "good old days" -- and turned eventually into disbelief: could a time of such foodstuffs *ever* have existed in the Motherland? Had family members *ever* sat down to huge meat pies, sturgeon in aspic, mounds of crayfish, souffles and babas? Had there *ever* been a time when there was so much caviar that it was used to clarify beef bouillon and then thrown away?

Even though the servants certainly weren't eating these delicacies, they did have access to abundance: pirogi (a kind of pie), kasha (grains), shchi (cabbage soup), kvass (a beverage fermented from black bread), beets, potatoes, roast goose, duck, pork, and beef, many varieties of fresh, dried and marinated fish, sauerkraut, sausage, and pickles. These staples became harder and harder to find after the Revolution, even with the exalted "progress" advertised on a yearly basis by Lenin, Stalin, et seq. Twentieth Century modernism that never quite made it from revolutionary tome to actuality.

Tamara, our Russian expatriate, urged us to incorporate many of the recipes as regular fare at the Quilt Inn. I think not. Not because we are not adventurous, but rather because the cookbook presupposes a completely different way of life than we are used to nowadays. Molokhovets assures us that we, too, can have fresh pears from our orchard in the middle of winter. How? According to the *Gift*, each pear, carefully culled, was placed in its own small individual copper saucepan with a lid, and laid in the icehouse. (We don't have one of those either.) Every two weeks a servant wiped off each and every pear, and the saucepan it rested in. (You can understand a people who rose up and demanded a revolution, if only to be taken off pear cleaning detail!)

And even more, close to the house was a storeroom of vast size, used to hold food for the almost-always huge family, guests, and hangers-on. Mushrooms were grown in the basement. Lemons were lined up on the shelves, none touching a sister, each to be wiped dry once a week. Kegs of sauerkraut had to be poked once a week with a pole to allow the dangerous buildup of methane gases to escape. (Horrors, if you missed a week of keg-poking...Boom! Death by sauerkraut!) Cauliflowers strung from the ceiling needed constant attention, and the windows were opened each morning and closed each evening. Even bacon had to be constantly rotated. And the cook slept in the kitchen, on a fold-out bed covered with a seaweed mattress. This was necessary because cook was always preparing for the next repast: a simple dinner took 24 hours to prepare.

You may disagree, but our feeling is that a cookbook like *A Gift to Young Housewives* is to be enjoyed as armchair travelling to the past, not as a "how to" for the present. Thank you, Tamara, for sharing this wonderful nostalgic vision, that is exotic, thought-provoking, unsettling, and for forcing us to remember what was, and why it isn't that way anymore.

✳ ✳ ✳

Here are some of our favorite cabbage recipes, otherwise known as "coleslaw calamities"...

Cabbage Pilaf

1 Onion, chopped
1 c long-grain Rice
3 c Cabbage, chopped
3 tbsp Tomato paste
3 tbsp Olive oil
2 c Water
1/2 tsp Caraway seeds
1/4 c fresh Parsley, chopped

Heat oil in saucepan. Saute onions and rice on medium heat, until onions are soft. Add cabbage. Stir until cabbage wilts. Stir in tomato paste, water, parsley, salt and pepper to taste. Bring to boil, cover and simmer 30 minutes or until liquid is absorbed.

Cabbagepatch Pork Chops

8 thick-cut Pork chops
1 medium Cabbage, shredded
2 tbsp Butter
2 cloves, Garlic, minced
1/4 c Onions, chopped fine
1/2 c white Wine *
1 c heavy Cream
2 Bay leaves
2 tbsp Bread crumbs
4 tbsp Parmesan cheese
2 tbsp melted Butter

Preheat oven to 350F.

Shred cabbage and blanch in boiling water for 5 minutes. Drain well. Saute garlic and onions in butter until soft. Add cabbage and seasoning. Cook 5 minutes. Set aside.

Season pork chops. Saute meat until brown on both sides. Set aside. Discard fat from pan and deglaze with wine. Reduce liquid to 4 cups (of course, we're not sure how you measure this: get yourself a serf from pear cleaning duty) and mix with cabbage. (That's the liquid, not the serf!)

Spread one-third of the cabbage mixture in casserole or deep glass baking dish. Layer four chops on top; one-third more cabbage; four more chops and remaining cabbage.

Warm cream in saucepan. Add to casserole. Place bay leaf on top. Bake, covered, for 1 1/2 hours. Remove bay leaf and discard. Mix breadcrumbs, cheese and butter and sprinkle over casserole. Bake, uncovered, for 30 minutes or until brown and crusty.

* For a colorful variation, use red wine and red cabbage.

Stuffed Cabbage

1 head Cabbage
1 lb lean ground Beef
1/2 lb lean ground Pork
3/4 c cooked wild Rice
1 can Tomatoes
1/2 c Tomato sauce
1/2 c green Onions, chopped
1 c Water
1/4 c brown Sugar
1 1/2 c Sauerkraut, rinsed and drained
1/3 c Raisins
1/2 tsp Thyme
1 tsp Caraway seeds
1 tsp Salt
1 tsp ground Ginger
1 tbsp Lemon juice
Fresh ground Pepper to taste

Core cabbage and cut in strips. Steam cabbage leaves until tender (about 5 minutes). Rinse in cold water, drain and set aside.

Combine beef, pork, rice, green onions, caraway seeds, thyme and pepper in large mixing bowl. Mix thoroughly.

Stir tomatoes, water, tomato sauce, raisins, brown sugar, lemon juice and ginger together in another mixing bowl.

Place cabbage leaves one at at time on work surface. Spoon 1/2 cup meat filling into center of leaf. Fold up bottom edge to cover filling. Fold in sides, then roll the filled part onto the top. Repeat with remaining leaves and filling.

Spoon 1 cup of sauerkraut into ovenproof casserole or shallow dish. Arrange cabbage rolls on top, with "seams" down. Top with remaining sauerkraut. Pour tomato mixture over cabbage. Cover and bake for 2 hours.

Better "Red" Than Dead Cabbage

1 red Cabbage
1 Onion
4 tbsp Lard or Shortening
4 sour Apples, cored and diced
6 Cloves
1/2 c Water
2 tbsp Vinegar
1 Bay leaf

Slice cabbage and onion. Saute onion in lard until slightly brown. Add cabbage and cook for 5 minutes. Add apples and other ingredients. Simmer for 1 1/2 hours.

Cabbage and 'Shrooms

1 Cabbage, chopped
1 Onion, chopped fine
2 c fresh Mushrooms
2 tbsp Sour Cream
Butter
Salt and fresh ground Pepper to taste

Steam cabbage for 5 minutes. Saute onion in butter, add mushrooms and saute another 5 minutes. Add cabbage and continue cooking until flavors blend. Just before serving stir in sour cream.

Bullwinkle and Boris' Borscht

2 lb Beets
3 c red Cabbage, shredded
2 c navy Beans
2 Carrots, peeled and diced
2 Leeks, slices
1 Parsnip, peeled and diced
1 Onion, chopped
2 lb beef Shortribs
2 c plum tomatoes, chopped
6 c beef Stock
3 c Water
6 cloves Garlic
1 tbsp fresh Dill
2 tbsp Tomato paste
4 c Chicken broth
2 tsp Caraway seeds
Salt and fresh ground Pepper to taste
4 tbsp Olive oil
1/4 c Lemon juice
Sour cream for garnish

Place beets in soup pot, cover with water and bring to a boil. Simmer 40 minutes or until tender. Remove beets with slotted spoon, reserve liquid. Remove beet skins, grate coarsely and set aside.

Sear shortribs in oil for 15 minutes or until brown. Pour off grease. Add ribs to soup pot and add beef stock, water, onion, garlic, and dill. Bring to a boil, reduce heat and cover. Simmer 1 hour. Add cabbage, beans, carrots, leek, parsnip, tomato paste, chicken stock and 2 cups of reserved beet liquid. Cover and bring to boil, reduce heat and simmer 15 minutes. Add caraway seeds, salt and pepper, tomatoes and reserved grated beets. Simmer another 15 minutes.

Remove ribs from broth. Remove meat from bones, discard bones. Return meat to broth. Add lemon juice. Return to heat, heat thoroughly. Serve with dollup of sour cream.

Pasta Cabbage Please

1/2 head Cabbage
4 oz Pasta (linguini or spaghetti)
1/3 c green Onions, chopped
4 tbsp Butter
1/2 Chicken stock
Salt and fresh ground Pepper to taste

Cut cabbage into strips. Break pasta into short lengths and cook in boiling water until tender. Rinse in cold water, drain well.

Melt butter in saucepan. Add cabbage. Cover and cook over medium heat until tender but still crisp. Add the pasta and stock. Stir over low heat until heated through. Season to taste and add green onions. Serve immediately.

Cabbage in the Bac Room

1 lb Bacon, cut in pieces
2 c Onions, chopped
1 head Red Cabbage, chopped fine
2 tart Apples, cored and cubed
1 c Raisins
3/4 c red Wine
3/4 c red wine Vinegar
2 tsp Caraway seeds
1 tsp Thyme
Salt and fresh ground Pepper to taste

Cook bacon in large pan over low for 15 minutes. Add onions and cook until softened. Add remaining ingredients and stir well. Cover and cook over medium for 1 hour, stirring occasionally. Adjust seasonings and serve hot.

Tamara's Mother's Savory Cabbage Strudel

Strudel dough:
1 1/2 c all-purpose Flour
1/4 tsp Salt
1 Egg
1/4 to 1/2 c warm Water
2 tsp Vinegar
Preheat oven to 400F.

Sift flour and salt together in bowl. Beat egg with water or milk and vinegar. Work liquid into flour mixture by hand to form dough. Knead on floured board until dough is no longer sticky. Place in bowl, cover and let stand for 30 minutes.

Roll dough as thin as possible. Stretch the dough gently from the center. This should make about 2 yards square of very thin dough. Brush with melted butter.

Filling:
4 lbs Cabbage, shredded
1 1/2 c heavy Sour cream
1 tsp Caraway seed
4 Eggs, hard-cooked and chopped

Steam cabbage for 5 minutes, and blanch. Press out excess moisture on paper towels. Mix with sour cream, caraway and eggs.

Sprinkle filling over dough and roll loosely as the dough will expand. Slide onto greased baking sheet. Brush with melted butter and sprinkle with water. Bake for 20 minutes at 400F, then reduce heat to 350F. Brush strudel again with butter and bake 10 minutes more or until golden brown. Remove from oven and dust with confectioners' sugar.

Cabbage Casserole

3 c Cabbage, shredded fine
1 1/2 c stewed Tomatoes
1/2 tsp Salt
1/2 tsp Paprika
2 tsp brown Sugar
Bread crumbs, fine
Parmesan cheese, grated

Preheat oven to 325F

Steam cabbage for 5 minutes. Drain well and pat dry with paper towels. Cook tomatoes, salt, paprika and sugar in saucepan. Butter a casserole dish. Layer with cabbage, and tomato mixture alternately. Sprinkle with Parmesan cheese mixed with bread crumbs. Bake for 30 minutes or until top is golden brown.

Cordon Bleu Cabbage

1 large head Cabbage

Trim loose outer leaves from cabbage. Cut out stem and enough cabbage to make deep well.

Filling:
2 c cooked ground Ham
1 c Bread crumbs
3/4 c hard Cheese, grated
1/2 tsp dry Mustard
Salt to taste
1/2 tsp Paprika
Dash cayenne

Mix all ingredients in mixing bowl. Fill center of cabbage with filling. Steam for 1 hour or until tender, making sure pot does not boil dry. Wrap cabbage in heavy foil and bake at 325F for 2 hours.

Cheese sauce:
3 tbsp Butter
3 tbsp Flour
1 1/2 c Milk
1 c Cheese, grated
1/4 tsp Salt
1/4 tsp Paprika
1/2 tsp dry Mustard
Dash cayenne pepper

Melt butter in saucepan. Stir in flour and blend. Slowly stir in milk and bring almost to a boil. When sauce is smooth and hot, reduce heat and stir in cheese and seasonings. Stir until smooth.

Number One [Sharp] Coleslaw

8 c Cabbage, shredded
1/2 c Vinegar
1/2 c Sugar
2 tbsp Sugar
2 tbsp Onion, chopped fine
1 tsp Salt
2/3 c Vegetable oil
Paprika

Combine all ingredients and toss to coat cabbage. Cover and chill overnight. Garnish with parsley before serving.

Number Two [Creamy] Coleslaw

8 c Cabbage, shredded
1/4 c Celery, chopped fine
2 Eggs, beaten
2 tbsp Sugar
1 tsp dry Mustard
1/4 tsp Salt
1/4 tsp fresh ground Pepper

2 tbsp Butter
1/2 c Vinegar
1/2 c whipping Cream

Combine cabbage and celery. Set aside.

Mix eggs and sugar in saucepan, blending well. Combine mustard, salt and pepper to egg mixture. Add butter and slowly stir in vinegar. Cook over low until mixture thickens. Remove from heat and chill.

Add whipping cream to chilled mixture, stirring well. Pour sauce over cabbage, toss well. Chill and serve.

Number Three [Vinaigrette] Coleslaw

1 Cabbage, shredded
2 green Peppers, sliced in rings
1 Onion, sliced thin and separated
2 c Vinegar
1 c Vegetable oil
1 c Water
1 c Sugar
1/4 tsp Salt
1/2 tsp fresh ground Pepper

Combine cabbage, green pepper and onion in large bowl. Mix well and set aside.

Combine remaining ingredients. Stir into cabbage mixture. Cover and chill overnight.

Red Cabbage and Sausage

1 head red Cabbage, cored and shredded
2 lb smoked Sausage, diced
2 Onions, sliced thin

Quilt Inn Country Cookbook

2 green Apples, peeled, cored and diced
2 tbsp Butter
1/3 c Vinegar
1/2 c chicken Stock
1 tsp Curry Powder
1/2 tsp Marjoram
Salt and fresh ground Pepper to taste

Brown sausage in butter in deep sacepan over medium-high heat. Add onion and cook until tender, about 10 minutes. Stir in cabbage, apples, vinegar, stock, curry powder, marjoram, salt and pepper. Cover and simmer on medium for 30 minutes.

We can't leave this chapter without a good recipe for...

Non-Exploding Sauerkraut

9 c Cabbage, shredded
1/4 c Pickling salt

Wash and shred cabbage. Measure 9 cups in mixing bowl. Mix with pickling salt. Let stand for 2 hours. Rinse, drain and rinse again. Pack wet cabbage into sterilized jars. Pack firmly so that liquid rises and covers cabbage. Leave 1 inch space at top of jar. Fit a piece of plastic wrap onto top of cabbage so air does not reach it. Seal jar with lid, but do not tighten -- this allows fermentation gases to escape -- eliminates need to "keg poke", and explosions!

Store at 68-72F to enhance fermentation process. Check occasionally and remove any scum that appears on surface of cabbage. (Scum won't form if plastic wrap is tight enough.) Fermentation will stop after 2 - 6 weeks.

Sauerkraut is ready when no bubbles appear on the surface and jar does not hiss when opened. If kraut is too salty for your taste, rinse it before using or serving. Store sauerkraut in refrigerator.

Pineapples are a traditional sign of welcome and often appear on country inn signs. "Pineapple" quilt block designs may be appliqued realistic renditions such as this, or may be more modern representational designs.

It's All Greek to Me

One of our favorite quotes from *Zorba the Greek* goes, "What I eat I turn into work and good humor." Whether it's in song, dance, or food, Greeks love to share their joyful spirit. This would be called a *joie de vivre*, but of course, that's an entirely different language, so instead, that phrase having already been taken, it's called *philoxenia*.

A friend from the old neighborhood, where we lived before the Quilt Inn days, came by to stay with us. George Spirodopolous brought Christina, his wife, and Little Georgio (who was at this time, five years older, a foot and a half taller, and more worried about girls than when we had last seen him!) It wasn't long before they had commandeered the Inn kitchen, and several volunteers, to prepare some Greek specialties for our lucky guests.

The emphasis of Greek food is simple preparation and wholesome ingredients which make it perfect "country cooking" for The Quilt Inn. And, it is relatively unchanged since Archestratus wrote the very first cookbook over 2,000 years ago.

Unfortunately, it was not a best seller. Since every recipe had to be chiselled on pieces of slate ("carved in stone" we refer to it today), the book not only took many decades to complete, but weighed more than the average Greek's cupboard could hold. Can you imagine checking it out of the Romus Librarius? ("Two days overdue, eh Spiros? Get your hernia fixed: you have a date with the lions!")

Two things we discovered about Greek food from George and his family: first, much of the food is prepared with olive oil, which in today's health-conscious eating is very good because it holds cholesterol levels down; and two, the food keeps extremely well, not only providing great leftovers but often tasting better the second time around.

Legend has it that Greek food is so aromatically delicious that one can swoon in ecstasy. Me, I thought it was the amount of garlic in many dishes!

So, George, Christina, and Little Georgio wish you *bon appetit* ...no, no, there we go again... they wish you *Kali Orexi!*

* * *

Appetizers (mezethes) are meant to be sampled sparingly, with ouzo as an accompaniment. Michael and I, in the early days of our marriage, used to go to our favorite Greek restaurant and eat a whole meal just from the appetizer list!

Tzatziki

2 c plain Yogurt
1 Cucumber, peeled and chopped fine and drained
5 cloves Garlic, crushed
Salt and fresh ground Pepper to taste

Combine all ingredients in non-metallic bowl. Mix well and chill. If you like tzatziki really thick, drain the yogurt overnight through cheesecloth. Serve with chunky bread or rolls.

Saganaki

This is a very rich cheese appetizer. Small quantities go a long way. Cut chunks of goat cheese or any solid white cheese. There are several excellent Greek cheeses that are the best for this dish. Try Kasseri which is a mild Cheddar-like cheese, or Kefalograviera which is a Gruyere-like cheese, or Manouri which is an unsalted table cheese.

Dust cheese lightly with flour. Heat a cast iron skillet or griddle to medium heat. Add butter and fry the cheese until golden brown. Remove pan from heat.

Warm 1/2 ounce brandy, pour it over the cheese and light it carefully. Serve with a flourish! Yell *OPA!* (To Your Health!)

(Keep a fire extinguisher handy!)

You can also add slices of black Amphissa olives or sausage just before you flambe the Saganaki.

Keftedakia
(Our translation: Meatballs for the Gods!)

1/2 lb ground Beef)
1/2 lb ground Lamb) or any combination equalling
1/2 lb ground pork) 1 1/2 lb meat
1 Onion, chopped fine
4 cloves Garlic, crushed
1/2 c bread crumbs, fine
1 Egg, lightly beaten
4 tbsp fresh Mint, chopped fine
1/2 tsp Oregano
Salt and fresh ground Pepper to taste
Flour
3 tbsp Olive Oil

Combine meat, onion, garlic, bread crumbs, egg, mint, oregano, salt and pepper in bowl. Mix well. Shape into 1 inch balls. Dust meatballs lightly with flour. Fry in olive oil until evenly brown.

Serve with toothpicks for party fingerfood, or with tzatziki and bread for an appetizer.

To serve as a main course, form meatballs into larger oval, sausage-shapes on skewers. Grill on medium heat until cooked through, about 20 minutes. Serve on bed of shredded lettuce, with tomato salsa and thinly sliced onion.

George tells me that the white chef's hat that customarily is worn in most kitchens of many fine restaurants, had its origins in Greece. It seems that the shape is based on Greek monks' hats. Chefs used to seek refuge in the monasteries to avoid persecution (when one of their recipes really went bad!) In any event, the different colors made it easy to tell who was a monk and who was a chef, so that there was no monk-eying around.

Classic Greek Salad

1 c Feta cheese, crumbled
3 large ripe Tomatoes, cut in chunks
1 large Cucumber, peeled, cut in chunks
1 small red Onion, sliced thin
2 dozen black Amphissa olives, pitted
3 tbsp Olive oil
1 tsp Oregano
Salt and fresh ground Pepper to taste

Combine tomatoes, cucumber, onion and olives in bowl. Sprinkle with oregano, salt and pepper. Drizzle oil and toss. Place in serving bowl or individual plates. Sprinkle with feta cheese.

There are many fine olive oils now available in regular grocery stores. The important thing to look for on the label is "extra virgin". This term means the oil was pressed out of the olives in the original old-fashioned way, often manually. This is the best olive oil. You may also see "pure" olive oil, which means the oil was pressed mechanically and with heat used to obtain maximum yields, a good oil, but not the best. This is OK, but heat destroys the fine subtle flavor and quality of the oil and should never be used in processing olives.

Try different brands of olive oil because, unlike our plain old vegetable oils, they vary greatly in taste, depending on the kind of olives used, and like wine, depend on the soil they grew in and the year; weather will change the moisture and ripeness of the olives. Many well-stocked Greek, or Italian, kitchens will have several different grades and flavors of olive oils, to be used for specific purposes.

Opa Okra!

2 c ripe Tomatoes, blanched and peeled
1 lb fresh Okra *(frozen could be substituted)*
2 medium Onions, chopped fine
3 tbsp Olive oil
1/4 c fresh Parsley, chopped
1/4 tsp Sugar
Juice of 1 Lemon
1/2 c red Wine
Salt and fresh ground Pepper to taste

Wash and dry okra. Cut off stems, not exposing seeds.

Heat oil in pan. Add onion and garlic, saute until lightly brown and fragrant. Stir in okra, tomatoes, parsley, sugar, lemon juice, wine, salt and pepper. Bring to a boil, cover and simmer on low for 30 minutes or until tender. Transfer to serving dish.

As every gardener knows you can never have too many zucchini recipes, because you can never get rid of all the zucchini that you can grow! The green thumb rule is: if you grow zucchini, no one leaves the property with anything less than a basket-ful!

Zorba's Zucchini

5 large ripe Zucchini *(give away another 5 to your neighbor)*
5 large ripe Tomatoes, sliced
1/2 c Olive Oil
1 1/2 c Feta cheese, crumbled
1/2 c fresh Parsley, chopped
1/2 c white Wine
Salt and fresh ground Pepper to taste

Preheat broiler.

Wash and dry zucchini, slice lengthwise. Brush with oil and place on baking sheet. Broil until golden brown. Set aside.

Grease shallow casserole. Layer zucchini, tomatoes, onion, feta, parsley, salt and pepper. Top with feta. Add wine. Bake at 375F for 30 minutes or until top is slightly brown and bubbly.

Feta cheese is excellent with almost any green vegetable. The salty, nutty flavor brings out the best of even commonplace garden vegetables.

Rice Pilaf

1 lb fresh Spinach
1 Onion, chopped fine
1 c long-grain Rice
1 1/2 c Water
2 tbsp Olive Oil
1 tbsp Dillweed, or Oregano
Salt and fresh ground Pepper to taste

Wash and dry Spinach, tear into small pieces. Set aside. Heat oil in saucepan. Add onions, saute until soft. Add rice, saute for 3 minutes. Stir in water, dillweed, salt and pepper. Bring to a boil, add spinach and stir. Bring to boil, cover and simmer on low for 30 minutes or until liquid is absorbed. Transfer to serving dish.

If you went to an arts and crafts show in ancient Greece, you would be wiser to take along your favorite recipes instead of your rendition of "Alexander's Mother". Cookery was considered the greater of the fine arts because it brought more consistent pleasure. Sophocles, Aristotle, and the rest were indeed famous philosophers and teachers, but in ancient Greece, what was the profession of highest prestige? You're right: the cook. Perhaps if Archimedes, when he said, "Eureka, I have found it!" while sitting in his bathtub, had invented a decent recipe for Tzatziki, instead of finding his rubber duckie, he would be even more famous today.

Roast Lamb

6 lb Leg of Lamb
6 Potatoes, peeled, cut in chunks
6 cloves Garlic, chopped
6 tbsp Olive Oil
Juice of 1 Lemon
1 tbsp Oregano
2 c Red Wine
Salt and fresh ground Pepper to taste

Preheat oven to 400F.

Remove excess fat from lamb, wash and dry thoroughly. Score top and bottom of lamb, rub in garlic. Rub lamb with olive oil and place in roasting pan. Squeeze lemon juice over meat, sprinkle oregano, salt and pepper. Bake for 45 minutes in hot oven. Reduce heat to 325F, add wine. Continue roasting 30 minutes per pound. Baste frequently during roasting.

Add potatoes during last 1 1/2 hours roasting. Transfer to platter for serving. Serve with Opa Okra, and a full-bodied wine like Castel Danielis or Mount Ambelos.

Gerry Lamb's Soup

3 lb Lamb, cubed, fat removed
1 large Onion, quartered
3 Bay leaves
1/2 c Barley
1 1/2 c Onion, chopped fine
1 c Carrots, chopped
1 c Celery, chopped
1 c Potatoes or Turnips, chopped
1/3 c fresh Parsley, chopped
1/4 tsp Caraway seeds

Place meat in soup pot, cover with water. Bring to boil, skimming off froth as it rises. Add onion, bay leaves, salt and pepper, and barley. Bring to boil, reduce heat, cover and simmer for 1 hour. Add onion, carrots, celery, potatoes and caraway. Simmer another hour. Serve with crusty bread and a fine chilled Rose wine like Rosella for a light meal.

Lamb Stew with Greek Egg-Lemon Sauce

Because lamb is such a rich meat, the acidity of the spinach in this dish adds an excellent counterbalance.

3 lb lean Lamb, cut in cubes
2 large Onions, chopped
5 cloves Garlic, minced
Large bunch fresh Spinach
1/4 c long-grain Rice
1 c white Wine
1 c Water
3 tbsp Olive oil
3 tbsp Dillweed
Salt and fresh ground Pepper to taste

Trim fat from meat. Heat oil and sear meat in skillet until browned. Add onions and garlic. Saute until tender. Stir in water, wine, dillweed, salt and pepper. Bring to boil. Simmer, partly covered, for 2 hours, or until meat is tender.

Wash spinach and pat dry with paper towels. Remove stalks. Add spinach and rice to stew. Stir gently occasionally. Cook for 20 minutes or until rice is cooked and liquid is reduced. Reduce heat, but keep stew hot.

Egg-Lemon Sauce:
3 Eggs
1 tbsp Flour
Juice of 1 Lemon (depending on tartness required)
Hot stock from stew

Beat eggs lightly in a bowl. Sprinkle with flour and continue beating. Add lemon juice and beat until well blended. Continue beating while slowly pouring in about one cup of hot stock from stew pan until sauce thickens. When completely blended, pour sauce back into meat and vegetables. Stir gently and heat over low for several minutes, without boiling or sauce will curdle. Serve immediately.

Another delicious traditional Greek sauce is a rich sauce, made without cream, that is excellent on fish or vegetables.

Skordalia

6 cloves Garlic, minced
6 slices White bread without crusts
1/2 blanched Almonds, slivered
1/3 c Lemon juice
2/3 c Olive oil
2/3 c Water

Tear bread into large chunks. Place in mixing bowl and sprinkle with water. Set aside. Combine garlic and almonds in blender until smooth. Add bread, lemon juice, olive oil and dash salt. Blend until mixture has thick creamy consistency, thin with water or thicken with more bread, if necessary. Chill before serving.

To ensure that their fish was fresh, superstitious ancient Greek cooks often set out in boats lit with lanterns which attracted the fish. These lanterns were also believed to ward off the monsters of the deep, and therefore I suppose we can safely assume that Greek cooks also invented the first nightlight!

For lighter Greek fare, try these delicious seafood recipes.

Hearty Fish Soup

2 lb fish pieces *(cod, halibut, red snapper will do)*
1 large Onion, chopped
5 cloves Garlic, minced
1 ripe green sweet Pepper
1/4 c Olive oil
1 c Tomato sauce *(canned will do)*
3/4 c Water
1 c White wine
1/4 c fresh Parsley, chopped
1/2 tsp Thyme
1 tsp Oregano, crushed
2 Bay leaves
Fresh ground Pepper

Saute onion, garlic and sweet pepper in oil until tender. Add tomato sauce, water, wine, parsley, oregano, thyme, bay leaves and pepper. Cover, simmer for 15 minutes. Add fish and simmer another 15 minutes. Serve in bowls with crusty bread, and a light dry white table wine like Hymettus or St. Helena.

Baked Fish Casserole

2 lb fish chunks *(cod or snapper will do just for the halibut)*
1 large Onion, chopped
6 green Onions, chopped
4 cloves Garlic, minced

1 sweet Green pepper, cut in chunks
3 medium Potatoes, scrubbed and cut in chunks
3 Zucchini, sliced
3/4 c Olive oil
2 tbsp fresh Parsley, chopped
1 Bay leaf
1 tbsp Oregano
1 c Water
1/2 c white Wine
2 tbsp Butter
Salt and fresh ground Pepper to taste

Preheat oven to 350.

Saute onions, garlic, green pepper, potatoes, zucchini for 3 minutes, in small batches. Place vegetables in baking dish or casserole. Sprinkle on parsley, bay, oregano, salt and pepper. Add water and wine. Bake for 45 minutes uncovered.

Wash fish and pat dry thoroughly with paper towels. Dust with salt and pepper. Place on top of vegetables. Brush with butter, return to oven for another 45 minutes, uncovered. Serve with full-bodied white wine such as Robola.

Baked Shrimp Au Gratin!

1 1/2 lb large Shrimp
2 tbsp Lemon juice
3 c Tomato sauce
1 1/2 c Feta cheese
1/2 c Parmesan cheese

Preheat oven to 400F.

Peel and devein shrimp. Wash and dry thoroughly. Sprinkle with lemon juice. Place shrimp in casserole. Cover with tomato sauce. Sprinkle feta and parmesan cheese on top. Bake for 25 minutes or until cheese is bubbly.

This makes a great appetizer when prepared in individual ramekins. Serve with Demestica white wine.

George says that if you visit Greece, you often will see men sitting at outdoor cafes, sipping quantities of ouzo and playing with their Komboli, or worry beads. I'd be worried about going home too, with a snootful of ouzo under my chef's hat!

Many Greek pastries are legendary for their rich, honey-drenched sweetness. So instead, after a hearty Greek meal, we find these light spicy cookies to be an ideal ending along with fine coffee, and perhaps a little Sambuca.

Greek Spice Cookies

5 c Flour
1 c Butter
1/2 c Icing Sugar
1 Egg yolk
Zest of 1 Orange
1 c Orange juice
2 tsp Baking powder
1 tsp Baking soda
1/4 tsp Salt
1/2 tsp Cinnamon
1/2 tsp ground Cloves
1/2 tsp grated Nutmeg
1 c Walnuts, chopped fine

Preheat oven to 350F.
Combine 3 cups flour, baking powder, soda, salt, cinnamon, cloves and nutmeg. Cream butter in mixing bowl until fluffy. Gradually add sugar and egg yolk. Beat in orange zest and juice. Beat in dry ingredients gradually until stiff dough is formed. Add more flour if dough is sticky. Knead on floured surface.

Drop spoonfuls of dough on ungreased baking sheets. Bake for 30 minutes or until golden brown. Cool on wire racks.

Syrup:
2 c liquid Honey
1 c Water
1 Lemon, sliced

Combine honey, water and lemon in saucepan. Bring to boil. Lower heat and simmer for 10 minutes. Dip cookies in syrup, remove and place on wire racks. Sprinkle with chopped walnuts. Let cool.

Dr. Galen, a physician in 131 A.D., recommended that honey be used to stimulate the affairs of the heart. I think this is why baklava is so rich: your heart goes into overdrive when you bite into this delicious Greek dessert! So if you have the time and want to indulge, here you go:

Baklava

Preheat oven to 375F.

The Pastry:
1 lb Phyllo pastry *(frozen works well)*
1 lb melted Butter

Butter a shallow baking pan, or cookie sheet that has 1-inch deep lip all around. Place one sheet of phyllo on the sheet. Brush with melted butter. Add another sheet of phyllo and brush with butter. Repeat until six sheets have been layered and buttered.

The Syrup:
1 c liquid Honey *(for a different flavor, try half and half with Buckwheat honey)*
2 c Corn syrup
2 thick Orange slices
2 thick Lemon slices
1 tsp Vanilla

Combine all ingredients in saucepan. Simmer for 15 minutes or until mixture becomes thin and runny. Do not boil. Squeeze lemon and orange juice into mixture and discard slices. Let cool before stirring in vanilla. Set aside.

The Filling:
1 c Pistachios, chopped   )
1 c Pecans, chopped   ) or any combination of
1 c Walnuts, chopped   ) fresh nuts to equal 4 cups
1 c Almonds, chopped   )
3 tsp Cinnamon

Mix all nuts in a bowl with cinnamon.

Assemble the Baklava:
Sprinkle half the nut mixture on the prepared phyllo. Add six more phyllo layers, brushing each with melted butter. Sprinkle remaining nut mixture on top layer. Add six more phyllo layers, repeating procedure. Cut into bite-size squares or diamonds. Brush top with butter. Bake for 30 minutes. Lower heat to 325F and bake another 20 minutes or until golden brown.

Remove from oven and pour syrup over pastry slowly, allowing it to soak in. Set aside at room temperature for several hours before serving.

Lionhearts

Orphans are left on doorsteps. In baskets. In secrecy and embarrassment, and with sad entreaties to take care of the precious bundle inside. Here was another orphan to look after.

At least, that's how it felt when I went to the firehall last night to pick up a parcel. I wish the firemen would be more open about it and own up to it. There's certainly nothing to be ashamed about. Not anymore. Not these days. A lot of men have been caught doing it.

When I returned to the Inn, Michael and I carefully opened the plainly wrapped package and gently lifted out our treasure. A beautiful applique quilt! Yes, our firemen quilt. On the "q.t." Seven volunteer firemen get together every two weeks to eat pizza, drink beer, watch a ballgame...and quilt. You just never know what goes on behind closed doors, do you!

It all started five years ago after the terrible MacPherson fire. Three young children who should never have been left alone were trapped in the back bedroom of a rapidly collapsing house. By that strange power of coincidence or divine intention that places the right people at the right place when needed, Doug, one of the volunteers, heard the call go out over his car radio. He'd been out that evening to The Rib House bar and remembered seeing Sam and Jessie MacPherson partying it up late. He knew that meant the kids were home unattended as usual. Fortunately, he was only eight blocks away at the time. Unfortunately, he had no equipment with him and the firehall was on the other side of town. He also knew that the poor wood frame houses on this side of town were tinderboxes just waiting to go up.

Doug was the first on the scene and without even hesitating, he charged straight into the burning house. To this day no one knows, not even Doug, how he found the children. The house was literally collapsing behind him as he went toward the bedrooms. Smashing the back window he pushed two unconscious children out the window. Although neighbours saw him go in the front, no one was watching the back of the building. By the time he got the third child to the window and out, both he and the baby were on fire themselves. Holding the child, and dragging them away from the house, he rolled on the ground to put out the fire, and then staggered to the front yard where help finally saw him.

The burns and glass lacerations put him in the hospital for weeks. His hands were the most severely damaged. He underwent more weeks of rehabilitation therapy. And another person was in the right place at the right time. His therapist nurse happened to be a quilter, and as part of his hand therapy, she started him quilting to regain strength in his wrists and mobility in his fingers. He found it to be a soothing form of necessary exercise, and just kept doing it when he returned to work. No one was going to impugn this hero's masculinity, so it became an accepted, if peculiar, thing around the firehall.

Slowly, a couple of other guys became curious, then interested and finally hesitatingly, joined in. Now it's a regular, clandestine part of their routine. Burly, gnarled, scarred, big-knuckled hands around the frame. It must be the strangest quilting bee you could imagine. And I'm sure their talk must sometimes make the quilt blush.

Their quilts are usually appliques. Not flowers or gentle little things like ladies might produce, but strong and bold like you would expect from men with hearts like lions who face terrible, sudden and terrifying dangers. Their quilts are full of movement and life.

The problem became what to do with the finished quilts. Michael and I are honored to be able to help. You see, when you visit The Quilt Inn, after you pass through the front door the first thing you see is a quilt hanging from the railing of the landing at the top of the stairs in the front hall. At the bottom of the stairs, Bruno, an antique wooden carousel dog picked up an auction, stands guard.

The quilt is on display so that guests from all around the country can see it and are able to purchase raffle tickets. Each year, on the anniversary of the fire, Doug draws the winner, who receives this wonderful gift by special delivery. All the funds are given to the local hospital. Firemen, perhaps more than anyone else in the town, know the value of the care for human life that a community hospital gives.

By the way, the children are fine now. The older boy

wants to be a fireman too, just like the hero who saved his life. And Sam and Jessie McPherson are much chastened and at least more attentive parents.

And, except for the scars, Doug's hands are just fine. So's his heart.

* * *

It's tradition around any firehall that the men take turns preparing their "specialty" meals for the other men. Because they could be called to an emergency at any moment, their recipes tend to be easy to start, and stop, at any time. The fellas use convenience items like frozen or canned ingredients: we like to use fresh whenever possible. The food also keeps well on a low heat for prolonged periods or can be quickly reheated. They are hearty and scrumptious, too!

Turkey Pot Pie
With Fire Captain Herb's Fresh Crust

1/3 c Butter
1/2 lb Mushrooms, chopped
1 c Chicken stock
1/4 c Flour
2 c Milk
1/2 tsp dried Thyme
1/4 tsp Hot sauce (Tabasco does nicely)
4 c diced cooked Turkey
1/4 c diced Pimento
2 1/2 c frozen Peas & Carrots

Preheat oven to 400F and butter a 3 quart casserole dish.

Melt butter in large saucepan. Add mushrooms. Cook several minutes. Sprinkle with flour. Cook five minutes but do not brown. Whisk in chicken stock and milk. Bring to a boil.

Reduce heat. Add seasonings and salt/pepper to taste. Simmer gently, stirring occasionally, for 10 minutes. Add turkey, carrots and peas to sauce. Spoon turkey mixture into casserole.

Herb's Crust:

1 c all-purpose Flour
2 tsp Baking powder
1 tbsp chopped fresh Parsley
1 tbsp chopped fresh Dill
1/4 tsp salt
1/3 c Butter
1/2 c Milk

Sift together flour and baking powder, parsley, dill and salt. Cut in 1/3 c butter until it forms small lumps. Sprinkle mixture with remaining milk. Roll dough into a ball. Roll out dough on floured surface to fit top of casserole. Place dough directly on top of turkey mixture in casserole. Bake 30 to 35 minutes.

Sean's Irish Stew

6 medium Potatoes, peeled & cut thick
3 large Onions, peeled & cut thick
3 pounds lean boneless Lamb, cut into cubes
3 tbsp chopped fresh Parsley
1 tsp dried Thyme
Salt & Pepper to taste
Water to cover ingredients

Preheat oven to 300F.

Sear lamb cubes in pan to seal in juices, remove from pan; brown onions and deglaze browning with a little water.

Arrange layers of potatoes, onions and lamb in large ovenproof casserole, sprinkling layers with seasonings. Add water to cover. Bake for 2 to 3 hours or until meat is tender.

Serve with Irish Soda Bread. *(Or some Irish "soda".)*

Irish Soda Bread

1 c all-purpose Flour
2 tsp Baking soda
1 1/2 tsp Salt
1/4 c Butter, softened
3 c whole wheat Flour
1 2/3 c Buttermilk

Preheat oven to 400F and grease (round) loaf pan.

Sift all-purpose flour together with baking soda and salt in large mixing bowl. Cut in butter with pastry blender until mixture forms coarse crumbles. Stir in whole wheat flour, mixing well. Add buttermilk, stirring until ingredients are thoroughly moistened.

Place dough on floured surface and knead for 5 minutes. Shape dough into round and place on baking pan. Cut 1/2-inch deep cross on top of loaf with sharp knife. Dust cross with flour. Bake for 40 minutes or until bread sounds hollow when tapped. Remove and cool on wire rack.

Backdraft Chili

2 tbsp Vegetable Oil
2 large Onions, chopped
2 cloves Garlic, minced
2 tbsp Chili Powder
1 tsp Paprika
1/2 tsp Oregano
Pinch hot red chili flakes, to taste
1/2 lb lean ground Pork
1/2 lb lean ground Beef
1 sweet red Pepper, diced
1 sweet green Pepper, diced
2 stalks Celery, diced
2 tbsp all-purpose Flour
1 c Milk

1 tin plum Tomatoes, drained
1/4 c Tomato paste
1 tin diced (mild) green Chilis
1 tin red Kidney Beans, drained
Salt and pepper to taste

Heat oil in large skillet. Cook onions and garlic until tender. Add chili powder, paprika, oregano and hot red chili flakes. Cook 1 minute. Add pork and beef. Cook until meat loses its raw appearance. Drain off excess fat. Stir in red and green pepper, celery and flour. Cook 2 to 3 minutes. Stir in milk. Bring to a boil. Reduce heat, cover and cook over low heat for 20 minutes. Add tomatoes, stir in tomato paste, mild chilis and beans. Cook 10 minutes longer, uncovered, until thick. Season with salt and pepper.

Serve over rice with sour cream or unflavoured yogurt. Garnish with grated cheese and diced avocado.

Firefighter Chicken Stew

2 medium Onions, sliced
1/2 c Carrots, sliced
1/2 c Celery, sliced
3 tbsp Butter
4-pound Chicken, cut up
1 c Yogurt
1 tbsp Curry powder
1 clove Garlic, minced
1 tsp Turmeric
2 tsp Salt
2 qt Water

In large saucepan, saute onions, carrots and celery in butter until soft. Add chicken and cook 20 minutes, turning pieces until they turn brown. Stir in yogurt, curry powder, garlic, turmeric and salt. Cook another 20 minutes on lower heat so as not to burn the yogurt. Add water, cover and simmer 1 hour or until chicken is tender. Uncover to thicken stew. Serve over rice.

Doug's Beef Stew

1/2 c Corn Starch
2 tsp Salt
1/4 tsp Pepper
1/2 tsp Paprika
1 1/2 lb lean stewing Beef, cubed
3 tbsp Vegetable Oil
1 1/2 c Carrots, cubed
5 small Potatoes, cubed
4 small Onions, quartered
3 stalks Celery, sliced
2 c green Beans, sliced
1 can Cream of Mushroom soup
1 pouch dry Onion Soup Mix
1 tbsp Worcestershire Sauce
1/2 tsp gravy Browning
1 3/4 c Milk

Preheat oven to 450F

Combine corn starch, salt, pepper and paprika. Dust meat cubes with mixture, reserve remaining mixture. Toss meat cubes with oil in ovenproof casserole. Bake uncovered for 30 minutes, stir occasionally. Add carrots, potatoes, celery, onions and green beans to meat.

Combine reserved cornstarch mixture with mushroom soup, onion soup mix, worcestershire sauce and gravy browning. Gradually stir in milk. Pour over meat and vegetables. Reduce oven to 350F. Bake, covered, for 1 hour. Remove cover and stir to combine ingredients. Return to oven, bake, covered for 45 minutes or until meat and vegetables are tender.

Southern Chicken Stew

3 - 3 1/2 lb Chicken, cut up
1 tsp Salt
6 Potatoes, peeled and quartered
2 cans Tomatoes, chopped, with juice
1 Onion, chopped
1 tsp Sugar
1 tsp fresh ground Pepper
1 lb Lima beans *(frozen will do; 20 oz package)*
1 lb whole kernel Corn *(frozen will do; 20 oz package)*

Place cut up chicken pieces and salt (*) in large pot with enough water to cover. Bring to a boil. Reduce heat, cover and simmer for 45 minutes or until chicken is cooked through. Remove chicken from broth. Remove meat from bones, cut into small pieces and set aside.

Add potatoes to broth and cook for 20 minutes or until potatoes are tender. Mash potatoes in broth for thickening. Re-add chicken, tomatoes, onion, sugar and pepper. Cook, uncovered over medium heat for 45 minutes. Add lima beans and corn and cook additional 15 minutes or until lima beans are tender.

(*) A Rule of Thumb for cooking meat with or without salt. Salt will draw the flavor out of meat and into the broth, so if you want a tasty broth, add salt in cooking the meat. But if you want tasty meat, do not add salt during the cooking; add any required salt afterward.

Stovetop Stew

3 lb Beef, cubed
2 1/2 c Onions, sliced
4 oz green Chilis
3 cloves Garlic, minced
1 tbsp fresh Ginger, minced
1/4 tsp Curry powder
1 tsp Salt
1 can Tomatoes

1 tbsp cider Vinegar
1 tbsp Lemon juice
1 tbsp Chili powder
1 12-oz can V-8 or any vegetable juice
2 tbsp Olive oil

Combine vinegar, lemon juice, chili powder and V-8 in bowl. Add meat and marinate up to 1 hour. Stir occasionally.

Heat oil. Saute onions, chilis and garlic over low heat until tender. Add ginger, curry and salt. Mix well and add tomatoes. Add meat and marinade to pan and simmer for 2 hours, stirring occasionally. Add water if liquid is necessary.

Serve with steamed rice or in bowls with crusty bread.

Hungry Hungarian Goulash

2 lb stewing Beef, cubed
1 c Onions, sliced
1 c Celery, sliced
1 c Carrots, sliced
1 c green Peppers, cut in strips
2 cloves Garlic, minced
4 tbsp Paprika
1 tsp Salt
1 tsp fresh ground Pepper
1 Bay leaf
3 tbsp Tomato paste
2 c Bouillon (or canned beef stock)
1/2 c Sour Cream

Sear meat in oil in large cast-iron pot. Remove meat. In pan juices, saute onion, garlic, green pepper and celery until tender. Stir in paprika, salt, pepper, bay leaf, tomato paste. Add bouillon and carrots. Return meat to pan. Bring to boil. Reduce heat and simmer, covered for 2 hours or until meat is tender and liquid is thickened.

Traditionally served with buttered noodles. Just before serving, stir in sour cream.

This is a modern abstract quilt design of a "Pineapple" plant, as if you looked at the plant from above and saw the layering of the scales on the skin of the pineapple. It is related to the "Log Cabin" block in that it is sewn by starting in the center and adding fabric row by row in strips.

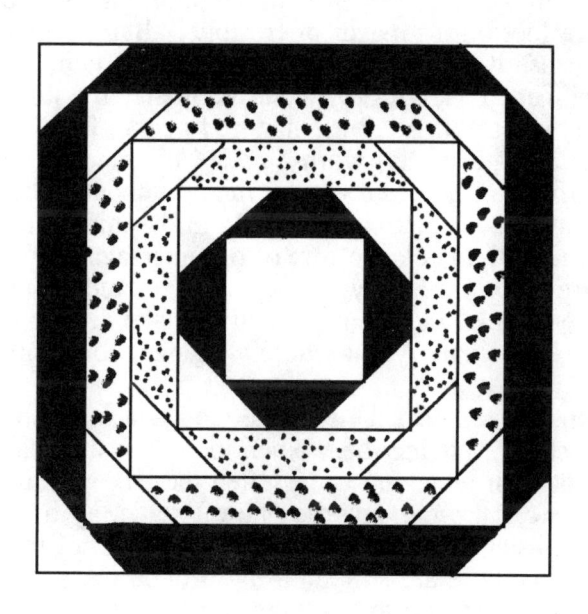

Loose Change

One of the things I love about the Inn kitchen is the stone floor. It's awfully cold, yes. On winter mornings you don't dare set bare foot on it for fear of frostbite. But it's great in the summer because it keeps the kitchen cool on the hottest days. The floor is made of large grey stone slabs that are still uneven and rough in most places. But a hundred years of feet working for hours in the kitchen has worn a noticeably smooth path around the room. The room looked funny without it, so we put a big old rough-hewn pine harvest table in the middle and surrounded it with an eclectic mix of old mismatched wood chairs. I grew up in a family that always gathered around the kitchen table to talk, and to laugh, and to make decisions, and sometimes even to eat. So, it's here we gather for "important" talk.

When couples visit the Inn, the men will often ramble off doing "guy stuff", leaving the women to gather informally around the harvest table and gab. Often the talk will turn to quilting and we share our favorite "how I made my first quilt" stories. As I listen, it often seems as if the spirits of the women who used to live here are still shuffling around the smooth worn stones, waiting their turn to tell their stories, too.

Sally Marie and Cal are a couple who visited the Inn a number of times. But Cal passed away last year. He had a wonderful sense of humor and great comic timing. We're going to miss him. So, for the first time, Sal is here by herself. She told us her story.

When Sally Marie got married, a long time ago, she was very young and there was little money to spend of any "extras" in life. Yet she was so proud of the fine young man she had married. He worked so hard and cared for her so much. And when young ones came along he was a strong and patient father no matter how dog-tired he was at the end of the day. So how could she dare want for more?

Every morning she rose early, long before Calvin woke up and she crept quietly out of the bedroom to start his breakfast. But one morning, she stopped briefly at the bureau, looked back at sleeping Cal and in a moment's inspiration, she silently scooped up half the pocket change that Cal had left there the night before. It was all of fifteen cents. A lot of money in those meager days. She couldn't take it all, she knew, but surely he wouldn't miss just *half* the change.

Cal said nothing that day, or evening. Sally felt a smug satisfaction that she was right. He hadn't noticed. So, the next morning she did the same thing again. And the next. Pretty soon, pennies at a time, she had collected the dollar she needed. She bought some fabric and needles and made her first quilt. So that was Sally's first quilt story.

But that was sixty years ago. And yet every morning since then Sally still helped herself to Cal's loose change. Some days there was a lot of change. Sometimes, when times were tough, there was not. Over the years Sally was able to provide many little extras for the family -- a special dress for the girls when needed, or a baseball glove for the boys. Cal often bragged on Sally to all their friends. What a wonderful housewife she was -- she could stretch her housekeeping allowance farther than anyone!

It just got to be a habit, even after they were comfortably off financially and Sal had emancipated access to all their money. There was something special about taking half of Cal's change every day.

Fifteen years ago, for their twenty-fifth wedding anniversary, Sally had her heart set on a trip to Arizona to see the Grand Canyon. Even though Cal had been laid off for several months, somehow there always seemed to be lots of change at the end of the day, to go into Sally's secret fund.

"You know Cal died last spring," she said finally, quietly. "I was right there at the end. You know, he was holding my hand. He looked me right in the eye and said 'Sal Gal'. He always called me 'Sal Gal'. He said, 'Sal Gal, keep the change!'. And he smiled that big stupid grin of his. That old fox! He knew all along. And he never said a word. Imagine that." She shook her head. "All those years, he never said a word."

Somehow it seems that great love is not in the important things you say, but in the little things that you never say.

Quilt Inn Country Cookbook

✱ ✱ ✱

Like in a marriage a little sauce goes a long way. And, can add a bit of extra zip to those otherwise humdrum foods or meals....

Having a number of good sauces up your culinary sleeve enhances your reputation as a gourmet cook in a very simple and easy way.

White Garlic Sauce

12 cloves Garlic, minced
2 lb Ricottta cheese (or cottage cheese will do)
1/2 c Parmesan cheese
1 c Milk
4 tbsp Butter
Fresh ground Pepper to taste

Heat milk and butter in saucepan. Add garlic and simmer but do not boil for 5 minutes. Add ricotta cheese and cook over low heat until cheese has melted. Remove from heat, stir in pepper. Serve over spinach pasta.

Red Garlic Sauce

6 c plum Tomatoes
1 small can Tomato paste
16 cloves Garlic, minced
4 tbsp Olive oil
2 Onions, chopped
4 tbsp Basil, chopped
3 tbsp Oregano, chopped
1/4 c Parsley, chopped
Fresh ground Pepper to taste

Saute onion and garlic in oil until tender. Add basil, oregano, and parsley. Cook for 3 minutes. Add tomatoes, tomato paste and pepper. Simmer partly covered for 1 hour. Serve over pasta, plain rice or fish fillets.

Green Garlic Sauce

1 lb Spinach, chopped fine
1 c Cottage cheese (or Ricotta)
1/4 c Parmesan cheese
8 cloves Garlic, minced
1/4 c Milk
Salt and fresh ground Pepper to taste

Melt butter in saucepan. Saute garlic until golden. Add spinach and cook for 5 minutes or until limp. Reduce heat, stir in cheeses and milk. Cook, while stirring, until cheese melts and mixture is cooked through. Serve over pasta or broiled chicken breasts.

And to prove that you can do ANYTHING with zucchini....

Zucchini Garlic Sauce

6 Zucchini, diced
12-15 cloves Garlic, minced
5 tbsp Olive oil
1 tsp Basil
1 tsp Oregano
1 tsp Thyme
Salt and fresh ground Pepper to taste

Heat oil in saucepan. Add garlic and zucchini. Cook on medium low heat for 5 minutes. Sprinkle with herbs and continue to cook until zucchini is pulpy. To serve, leave sauce slightly lumpy or mash it to form paste. Serve over grilled fish.

Horseradish and Sausage Sauce

3/4 lb Italian sausage, chopped, sauteed and drained
1/3 c fresh Horseradish, grated *(use more if you like extra hot)*
1/2 Onion, chopped fine
4 Tbsp Flour
2 c chicken Stock
4 Tbsp butter
4 cloves Garlic, minced
1/8 tsp Nutmeg
1 c Whipping cream
Dash Cayenne pepper
Fresh ground Pepper to taste

Melt butter and saute onion and garlic until golden. Add flour and mix well. Add stock and stir until thickened. Add pepper, cayenne, nutmeg and cream and bring just to a boil. Reduce heat and add horseradish and sausage. Heat through before serving. Serve over mashed potatoes or steamed vegetables.

Peppery Orange Sauce

1 hot red Pepper, chopped
3 green Onions, chopped
1/2 c Onion, chopped
3 cloves Garlic, minced
1 strip Orange peel
1 tbsp Lemon juice
2 tbsp Flour
1 c dry Red wine

Saute green onions in saucepan. Add orange peel, garlic, lemon juice and red pepper. Stir in flour. Stir in wine. Add 1 cup Water and simmer, covered, for 45 minutes, stirring occasionally. Pour over roast lamb 1/2 hour before end of cooking time, or use as "gravy" with broiled lamb chops.

Mustard Sauce

1/3 c Dijon mustard
2 c heavy Cream
1/3 c Vinegar
1/2 c Onion, chopped
10 Peppercorns
1/4 tsp Thyme
2 tbsp Olive oil

Saute onions in saucepan in oil until tender. Stir in peppercorns vinegar, thyme and bring to a boil. Remove from heat and stir in cream. Return to heat and cook until thickened. Remove from heat and discard peppercorns. Stir in mustard, butter and salt to taste. Serve over pork medallions.

Curry Sauce

1 Onion, chopped fine
1 cup Tomato sauce
2 c Water
4 tbsp Olive oil
3 tbsp Curry powder
1/4 tsp Salt
1/8 tsp Coriander
1/8 tsp Cumin seed
1/8 tsp dry mustard
1/8 tsp ground Ginger
1/8 tsp ground Mace
1/8 tsp ground Cloves

In mixing bowl, mix all spices; and add 1/4 cup water, stirring to make thin paste. In saucepan, saute onions in oil. Add spices to saucepan. Stir constantly to prevent burning, but allow mixture to turn brown. Add tomato sauce and remaining water. Blend until smooth. Cover and simmer for 1 hour. Add extra water to thin sauce if necessary. Serve over plain steamed rice to accompany pork chops.

Open Sesame Nutty Butter

2 sticks unsalted Butter, softened
1/4 c Sesame seeds, toasted
1/4 c green Onions, chopped fine
2 tbsp Sesame oil
2 tbsp Soy sauce
Fresh ground Pepper to taste

Blend all ingredients together until smooth. Spoon into individual ramekins or butter mold and chill until serving. Serve with grilled fish steaks.

Savory Fresh Herb Butter

1 stick unsalted Butter, softened
1 tsp fresh Tarragon
1 tsp fresh Thyme
1 tsp fresh Oregano
1/2 tsp Fresh ground Pepper
3 tbsp fresh Parsley, chopped fine

Combine all ingredients in a blender and process until well blended. Place in individual ramekins and chill before using as a table butter for warm home made bread or rolls. Let butter pats melt over steamed vegetables, when serving them "family style" (in one large bowl that everyone helps themselves from)

Tangy Orange Butter

2 sticks unsalted Butter, softened
2 tbsp Orange zest, grated
2 tbsp Cointreau
2 tbsp Orange juice (fresh is best)
2 tbsp confectioners' Sugar
1/4 tsp Vanilla extract
1/4 tsp Nutmeg

Blend butter, sugar and orange zest in mixing bowl. Slowly beat in liqueur, juice, vanilla and nutmeg until smooth. Spoon into individual ramekins or butter mold and chill until serving. Serve with hot breakfast muffins or on pancakes.

English Custard Sauce

(This is an exception to sauces adding flavor. The English have an interesting custom of adding a bland custard sauce to tasty desserts....?)

1 c heavy Cream
4 Egg yolks
1/3 Sugar
2 tsp Vanilla

Scald cream in saucepan over low heat. Beat egg yolks with sugar until lemon yellow colored. Add cream to eggs, stirring constantly. Transfer to saucepan and cook, but do not boil, over medium heat, stirring until thickened. Add vanilla. Serve hot or at room temperature. (Sauce will form crust as it cools, so cover it tightly with plastic wrap.) Very nice over strong flavored berry desserts.

Hot Toddy Rum Sauce

1/4 c dark Rum
1/2 c Butter
1 c Water
1 c white Sugar

Heat sugar and water in saucepan until sugar dissolves completely and syrup thickens slightly. Remove from heat and add butter. Stir in rum. Return to heat briefly to heat through. Serve over plum pudding, spumoni ice cream or sliced bananas and cream.

Sunday, Sunday

In the town that lies close the the Inn, Sunday always arrives the same way. Regardless of the weather, the first light of dawn softens the everyday sharp contours of the empty town streets, and later, of the townspeople too. If you sleep with your windows open, and wake early enough, you can hear the bells ringing from the Church a mile away. There is a different feel to Sunday mornings, an almost ethereal stillness that allows itself to fold over the area only once a week. Even the news of the day, whether international, national, or the home-grown gossip variety, slows to a trickle, and people become more reflective.

Sunday is often called "the Sabbath" which derives from the Hebrew word "shabbat", which means "cessation" or "rest". A lot of people use Sunday to catch up on their sleep, and therefore emply, and enjoy, the literal meaning of the word. In the Judeo-Christian tradition, Genesis records the first Sabbath as a moment of Divine inspiration: "So God blessed the seventh day, and hallowed it, because on it God rested from all the work He had done in Creation". This is not fatigue, but rather the restful satisfaction of completion.

Yet, the true Sabbath transcends religious differences, and in fact may only be symbolic of the Sunday frame of mind: Jews and Seventh-day Adventists celebrate and repose between sunset Friday and sunset Saturday; Muslims on Friday; Buddhists on Sunday. Even those who don't consider themselves religious, have rituals they observe. Some read the Sunday paper, pouring over each item and feature with an unhurried thoughtfulness. Others go for a stroll in the park and feed the wildlife. Others visit with family and friends

At the Inn, we welcome all the diversities, as well as the similarities. One need only to be seeking good food, pleasant company and respite from one's normal day-to-day activities to enjoy brunch at The Quilt Inn. It's time they put aside for repose and renewal. As one of the locals said, "Coming to the Inn every Sunday is like a mental health day for me!" We're always glad that they do.

Sunday Brunch should be a leisurely, special meal. Unlike everyday breakfasts where one is hurrying on to other activities, and unlike lunch that is often, literally, "sandwiched" between appointments, brunch is an in-between sort of time of day, and should be a time to prepare slightly more elegant dishes, with time given to savor them.

* * *

Brunch should always start with fresh juice. It takes extra time to prepare but tastes so much better than any pre-packaged kind. If you don't like citrus juices like orange or grapefruit, try a vegetable juice like spicy tomato, or carrot if you're feeling venturesome.

I don't know why all the great, and famous, coffees, seem to originate in Europe. Perhaps they've learned the art of relaxing and truly savoring food and drink. Here are some morning coffee recipes to sip while you read the newspaper or think about what you're going to do today...

Viennese Coffee

For every cup of coffee, melt 1 ounce of semisweet chocolate with 1 tablespoon of heavy cream in the top of a double boiler. Gradually whisk in coffee until frothy. Pour into large coffee cups. Top with whipped cream and sprinkle with cinnamon or grated orange zest.

Belgian Coffee

For each cup of coffee fold 1 beaten egg white into 1 tablespoon whipped cream and put into bottom of coffee cup. Pour in hot coffee until cream floats to surface. Garnish with cocoa powder.

Quilt Inn Country Cookbook

Cafe Brulot

Combine 5 Cinnamon sticks, 3 strips of orange peel and 2 strips of lemon peel, with 1 teaspoon of allspice and 8 cubes of sugar in a chafing dish or skillet. Pour in 1 cup of Cognac and heat without stirring until the liquid is warm. Light the liquour with a match and stir until the flames die out. Pour in 6 cups strong hot coffee and stir. Strain and ladle into coffee cups.

But for those of you who prefer tea, the English are renowned for their fussiness when it comes to preparing a "proper" cup of "char". I lived in England for a number of years, perhaps long enough for them to convince me that it really does make a difference in the taste.

A "Proper" Cup of Tea

A really good cup of tea always starts with tea leaves. This has the added advantage of allowing you a much wider choice in the kind of tea you use. Just like wine, there are mild teas, mellow teas and really sharp, strong teas, and there are marvellous flavored teas. Just be sure you always warm the teapot first. Place your tea leaves loose in the pot -- one for each cup of tea, and "one for the pot".

Fill a kettle with fresh water -- never re-boil water for tea. Bring the water to a full rolling boil and pour it into the teapot. Cover for 5 minutes and let it steep.

Pour the tea through a fine mesh strainer into china cups. Tea should always be served in china cups, serving it in anything else is like serving beer in styrofoam cups.... Don't worry, china nowadays isn't always those delicate little flowery cups your Grandmother had a collection of. There are many modern, and manly, patterns and styles now to choose from.

Tea purists will demand their tea black, with perhaps a pinch of sugar to bring out the aromatic flavors. But for those who prefer a little milk in their tea, the "rule" is to pour the milk into the cup first, then add the hot tea. The tea then mixes itself, and believe me, it tastes different -- although there is no scientific reason why this should be so, that I know of. Just try it, it improves the taste.

* * *

Devilish Crab Puffs

24 small baked Puff Pastry shells
8 oz Snow Crabmeat
2 tbsp Butter
1 Onion, chopped fine
1/2 green Pepper, chopped fine
1 stalk Celery, chopped fine
1 tsp Curry powder
1 tsp dry Mustard or Dijon mustard
1 tsp Worcestershire sauce
1/4 tsp Salt
Dash Cayenne pepper
2 tbsp Flour
1/2 c Cream
fresh ground Pepper and Paprika to taste

Preheat oven to 350F

Melt butter and saute onion, pepper and celery until tender. Mix in curry powder, mustard, salt, pepper and cayenne. Cook gently for 2 minutes. Remove from heat and add flour and cream. Heat while stirring, bringing to boil and thickening. Add crab, Worcestershire sauce and paprika. Stir and bring to boil again. Mixture should have consistency of thick paste.

Spoon mixture into pastry shell and bake until heated through and golden brown. Serve with fresh garden salad and Russian dressing.

Basic Crepes Recipe

3/4 c Flour
Dash Salt
3 Eggs, beaten
2 tbsp melted Butter
3/4 c Milk or Buttermilk

Sift flour and salt together. Add beaten eggs and beat with wire whisk until smooth. Add butter and mix thoroughly. Add enough milk until batter has texture of heavy cream. Let stand 30 minutes, then beat again.

Heat non-stick pan or griddle to medium and brush with butter. Pour in tablespoon of batter to thinly cover the pan. When crepe browns, loosen and flip to other side.

To serve as a dessert, stuff with fresh fruit, and roll. Add dollup of whipped cream, or spoonful of fruit preserves, or fresh fruit puree.

To serve as a light lunch, make crepes slightly larger and fill with favorite stuffing, such as crabmeat or cheese and mushrooms. Serve with chutney and fresh garden salad.

For savory variations, add 1/3 cup of fresh parsley, dillweed or finely chopped green onion to the basic crepe batter and blend it thoroughly.

To serve as a hearty cold-weather meal, make 12 crepes dinner-plate size.

Stuffing:
1/2 c ripe Olives, pitted and chopped
1/2 lb spicy Sausage, sliced thin
2 lb Plum tomatoes, peeled
2 green Peppers, seeded and diced fine
1 clove Garlic, minced
2 tbsp Olive oil
1/4 tsp Salt
1/3 c fresh Parsley, chopped

Dash hot pepper flakes
3/4 c Parmesan cheese, grated

Saute garlic, onions and peppers until tender. Add tomatoes and cook 5 minutes, until most of the liquid has evaporated. Add remaining ingredients except parsley and cheese. Simmer 20 minutes or until thick. Stir in parsley.

Spoon 1/4 cup mixture and spoonful of cheese onto each crepe. Roll and transfer to baking sheet. Sprinkle with remaining cheese. Cover with foil and bake at 325F for 10 minutes or until cheese is melted and crepes are hot. Uncover and broil until cheese is golden brown.

Swiss Quiche with Seafood Sauce

1 unbaked Pie shell
4 Eggs yolks, lightly beaten
1 1/2 c light Cream
1/4 tsp Salt
1/8 tsp Nutmeg
4 Egg whites
1 1/2 c Swiss cheese, shredded

Preheat oven to 450F.

Bake pie shell until golden brown. Reduce heat to 350F.

Combine egg yolks, cream, salt and nutmeg. Beat egg whites until stiff, fold into yolk mixture. Fold in cheese, pour into pie shell. Bake for 45 minutes or until tester inserted into center comes out clean. Let stand 5 minutes.

Seafood Sauce:
Drain and flake 1 can crabmeat. Saute crabmeat in butter. Blend in 2 teaspoons of flour and a pinch of salt. Add 1 cup light cream. Cook while stirring until thickened.

To serve: pour sauce over slices of quiche and garnish with

cherry tomatoes sliced in two. Serve with a smooth and spicy Pinot Noir wine.

Ratatouille

1/2 lb fresh Mushrooms, sliced
1 Eggplant, cut in cubes
2 stalks Celery, sliced
1 red Pepper, chopped
2 zucchinis, sliced
2 green Onions, chopped (for garnish)
2 tbsp Sesame seeds, toasted (for garnish)
1/2 tsp Salt
6 tsp Sesame oil
3/4 c Chicken stock
2 tbsp Soya sauce
1 tbsp dry Sherry
1 tsp Cornstarch
2 tsp Garlic, minced
1 tsp fresh Ginger, minced
1 tbsp fresh Coriander, chopped

Preheat oven to 350F

Sprinkle eggplant with salt and let stand for 30 minutes.

Saute celery, onion and pepper in sesame oil in casserole until tender. Remove vegetables and set aside. Saute zucchini, muchrooms, and eggplant for 5 minutes or until soft. Add back the celery, onion and pepper, and remove from heat.

Combine stock, soya sauce, sherry and cornstarch in mixing bowl and blend well. Stir into vegetable mixture. Cover and bake for 40 minutes.

Stir in garlic and ginger. Recover and bake for additional 10 minutes. Stir in coriander and garnish with green onions and toasted sesame seeds before serving. Serve with a red Zinfandel wine.

Aliske Webb

Sunshine Stir Fry Salad

1 lb boneless Sirloin
2 tbsp Olive oil
3 cloves Garlic, minced
4 c mixed fresh salad Greens
2 Oranges, peeled and segmented
1 red Onion, peeled and sliced thin
1/2 Walnut pieces

Cut beef into thin strips. Heat oil and stir fry beef and garlic for 2 minutes. Remove with slotted spoon.

Arrange greens on four individual plates. Sprinkle with walnuts, onions and orange segments. Add beef at the last minute and drizzle with dressing to serve.

Vinaigrette Dressing:
1/2 c red wine Vinegar
4 tbsp Olive oil
4 tbsp Dijon mustard
4 tbsp Orange or Lemon juice

Combine all ingredients and chill until ready to use. Whisk briskly before serving.

Hearty Quilt Inn Salad

1 lb spicy smoked farmer's Sausage, chopped
1 lb fresh Mushrooms, sliced
1 c fresh Radishes, sliced
1/2 lb Provolone cheese, cut in strips
1 lb mixed fresh Greens (about 10 cups)

Fry sausage in skillet on high for 5 minutes or until browned. Remove sausage and drain on paper towels to remove excess fat.

Combine sausage, mushrooms, radishes, cheese and toss with greens.

Dressing:
2 tbsp Dijon mustard
3 tbsp red wine Vinegar
2 cloves Garlic, minced
2 tbsp Herbes de Provence *(see "Provence" page 134)* or any combination of fresh savory herbs
1/3 c Olive oil
1/3 c sour Cream

Whisk all ingredients together or blend in food processor until smooth. Toss with salad just before serving.

Asparagus Stir Fry

1 lb Asparagus, trimmed and sliced on diagonal
1/2 c fresh Peas
1/2 lb Snow peas
1 sweet red Pepper, seeded and sliced
1 sweet yellow Pepper, seeded and sliced
1/4 lb green Beans, trimmed and sliced on diagonal
1 Carrot, peeled and sliced thin on diagonal
3 green Onions, chopped
1/3 c fresh Coriander
2 c Basmati or Wild rice
2 tbsp Olive oil
3 cloves Garlic, minced
2 tbsp fresh Ginger root, chopped
1/3 c Vinegar
1 tsp Honey
1/2 tsp Salt
3 tbsp Orange juice
1 tsp Sesame oil

Rinse rice and place in saucepan with 2 3/4 c cold water. Bring to boil; reduce heat and cook uncovered until rice is cooked and is absorbed. Remove from heat and set aside.

Heat oil in large skillet, or wok. Add garlic and ginger, cook for 3 minutes until tender. Add carrots, cook 2 minutes. Add green beans, red pepper, yellow pepper and asparagus. Cook 2 minutes. Add peas; then snow peas. Remove from heat briefly.

Combine vinegar, honey, salt, orange juice and sesame oil. Stir into vegetable and return to heat. Stir in rice, green onions and coriander.

Serve immediately, as a side dish with lamb or fish or with pita bread as main dish. Goes well with a Beaujolais wine.

Sunday Salmon Souffle

4 Eggs, separated
1/2 c heavy Cream
4 tbsp smoked Salmon, slivered fine
1 tbsp fresh Chives, chopped fine
1/2 c Parmesan cheese, grated
1 tsp Lemon zest
1 tsp Cornstarch
Pinch salt
Fresh ground Pepper to taste

Preheat oven to 350F and lightly butter 6 individual ramekins. Coat inside of ramekin with grated Parmesan and set aside.

Stir together egg yolks, cream, salmon, chives, zest, cornstarch, salt and pepper in mixing bowl.

In separate bowl, beat egg whites with few drops of lemon juice until firm but not dry. Fold egg whites into yolk mixture.

Fill ramekins with souffle mixture and place on baking sheet. Bake for 10 minutes or until fluffy and golden. Serve immediately with salad and a Merlot wine.

A Lifestyle in Provence

We have these wonderful friends, Gail and Gerry, whose goal is also to own an Inn -- in the South of France. We hope their dream comes true, and in their honor, we include this set of recipes. It is largely on their tales of France and its beauty that we drew our inspiration. There is clearly, to those in love with this area, nothing quite like the country, the people, the smells, and the food of Provence.

When Charles de Montesquieu said, "If I were King I would close all cafes, for those who frequent them are dangerous hotheads!", we cannot believe that he would be referring to the people of this area, for they are far too sated (and sotted with French wine) to become hotheads about anything, except perhaps defending the *honneur* of the French chef.

Fresh herbs are an important part of Provencal cooking, which also makes it ideal country inn fare. It is here that we learned not to cut herbs, but to tear them when using them in recipes. It brings out more flavor, and makes your fingers smell great! When herbs are out of season, use the best and freshest dried herbs you can find. A distinctive *Herbes de Provence* mixture can be recreated by combining one half cup each of thyme, bay leaf, rosemary, summer savory, lavender, cloves and orange zest. Mix them well and store in air-tight container. And when you serve any of these dishes, try a chilled rose.

Whatever you serve, remember the words of Jean Anouilh, who said, "Everything in France is a pretext for a good dinner."

* * *

Salade Nicoise

4 new Potatoes, baked
1 c green Beans, cut lengthwise, cooked and dried
2 ripe Plum Tomatoes
1/4 c black and green Olives
1 hard-boiled Egg
1 can Tuna
2 tbsp red Onion, chopped
1 tbsp Capers, drained
2 tbsp fresh lemon juice
2 tbsp extra virgin Olive oil
Fresh ground Pepper to taste
2 tsp fresh Rosemary, chopped
2 cloves Garlic, minced
3 tbsp fresh Parsley, chopped
Salt to taste
Lemon wedges

Place tuna in mixing bowl, breaking into chunks. Add onion, capers, 1 tablespoon lemon juice, 2 teaspoons of olive oil, and pepper. Toss gently with fork until well mixed. Set aside.

Cut potatoes into chunks and place in mixing bowl. Add 1 tablespoon olive oil, 1 1/2 teaspoons lemon juice, rosemary, garlic, pepper and salt. Toss and set aside.

Cut tomatoes into slices and place in bowl. Sprinkle with pepper, salt and 2 tablespoons of parsley. Toss beans with 1 tablespoon lemon juice and 1 teaspoon olive oil.

To serve: Place all ingredients in large shallow bowl or on large platter and serve with lemon wedges.

Quilt Inn Country Cookbook

Salade Provencal

12 small new potatoes
1/4 c extra virgin Olive oil
1/2 tsp Salt
2 tsp fresh ground Pepper
1 Duckling
1 Orange, halved
1/2 lb garlic farmers Sausage
1 whole Garlic head
3/4 c fresh Parsley, chopped
1/2 c red Onion, chopped fine
1/2 c black and green Olives
1 1/4 c Vinaigrette
1 medium Savoy Cabbage

Preheat oven to 400F

Prick potatoes with fork. Place olive oil in bowl and roll potatoes in oil. Sprinkle with salt and teaspoon pepper. Bake for 1 hour, uncovered, turning occasionally. Remove from heat. Let cool, and cut into chunks. Set aside.

Clean duck, rinse well and pat dry. Prick skin with fork. Rub duck with orange halves and sprinkle liberally with salt and pepper. Place duck in roasting pan, breast side up. Roast for 1 hour.

While duck roasts, cook sausages in 2 quarts water in saucepan. Bring to a boil, reduce heat and simmer for 40 minutes. Remove from water and let cool. Remove skin and cut into thick rounds. Cut rounds in quarters. Set aside.

Separate garlic cloves. Do not peel. Place in saucepan and cover with water. Bring to a boil, reduce heat and simmer 5 minutes. Drain, allow to cool and peel.

After duck has cooked, turn it over. Add garlic cloves to pan. Roast another 10 minutes. Transfer to platter and allow to cool. Remove skin and shred meat into chunks. Remove garlic cloves from pan and set aside.

Combine potatoes, parsley, red onion and olives to vinaigrette and toss gently. Add 1 teaspoon ground pepper. Add sausages, duck and garlic cloves. Fold all ingredients together gently. Serve on bed of cabbage leaves.

Barley Pilaf

1 Onion, chopped corase
2 Zucchini, diced coarse
6 cloves Garlic, chopped
6 ripe Plum tomatoes, seeded, chopped
1 c cooked pearl Barley
1 c Pine nuts, toasted
1/3 c Olive oil
1 c fresh Basil, chopped
1/4 c fresh Parsley, chopped
1/2 Chicken stock
Salt and fresh ground Pepper to taste

Heat oil in skillet and saute onion, zucchini and garlic until tender. Add stock and cook 2 minutes more. Add tomatoes, salt and pepper. Cook 1 minute, stirring frequently.

Add barley, pine nuts, basil and parsley. Stir well and cook until heated through. Serve immediately.

Nicoise Shrimp

1 lb Shrimp, cleaned and deveined
1/2 c Olives, pitted
1 Leek, washed and chopped
1 stalk Celery, chopped
3 tbsp Olive oil
1 c dry White wine
1 tbsp Tomato paste
1/2 c sun-dried Tomatoes, drained and chopped
4 cloves Garlic, minced
2 tsp Herbes de Provence mixture
Salt and fresh ground Pepper to taste

Saute leek and celery in oil over low heat until tender. Stir in wine and tomato paste and bring to a boil. Stir in shrimp, olives, sun-dried tomatoes, garlic and herbs. Increase heat to medium and cook until shrimp are cooked through. Serve immediately. Try it with a Pinot Blanc wine.

If you think plain old garden variety green beans are boring, try this...

Haricots Verts Provencal

1 lb fresh green Beans
1 Onion, chopped coarsely
6 cloves Garlic, chopped fine
4 Tomatoes, peeled, seeded and chopped
2 tbsp Olive oil
1/2 c dry white Wine
1/2 c pitted Olives
1 tbsp Lemon juice
2 tbsp fresh ground Pepper

Wash beans and cut ends off. Steam until tender but still crisp. Drain, rinse under cold water and set aside.

Saute onion and garlic in olive oil for 5 minutes. Add tomatoes and wine and cook for 20 minutes over medium heat. Toss in the beans and olives and heat thoroughly. Sprinkle with lemon juice and fresh ground pepper. Serve on platter with parsley garnish.

Waldorf Beans

1 lb fresh green Beans
6 strips Bacon, cut in chunks
1/2 c Roquefort cheese, crumbled
1 1/2 c Walnuts, toasted
Fresh ground Pepper to taste

Steam beans until tender but still crisp. Drain, rinse under cold water and set aside.

Cook bacon chunks in skillet over medium heat for 5 minutes or until well cooked. Remove from skillet and drain on paper towels. Remove excess fat from pan and add green beans to skillet and heat through. Add Roquefort and toss lightly for 1 minute or until cheese just begins to melt. Add walnuts and bacon and sprinkle with pepper. Serve immediately.

Nicoise Ratatouille

1 lb Zucchini, cubed
3 Tomatoes, diced
2 Leeks, washed, dried and cubed
1/2 c pitted Olives
1 Eggplant, cubed
2 tbsp Olive oil
1 tsp Salt
5 cloves Garlic, minced
1/3 c Pesto
Fresh ground Pepper to taste

Preheat oven to 350F.

Sprinkle eggplant with salt and set aside for 1 hour. Rinse, drain and pat dry with paper towels. Saute leeks and garlic in olive oil for 5 minutes. Add zucchini and cook another 3 minutes. Stir in tomatoes, olives, pesto, pepper and eggplant. Transfer to ovenproof dish. Cover and bake for 45 minutes, stirring occasionally.

Quiche de Nice, Sans Oeufs
(Without eggs)

1 pastry pie shell
2 tsp Dijon mustard

Brush mustard on pie shell; set aside.

Filling:
4 sweet red Peppers, cut into slices
2 tbsp Olive oil
2 Onions, chopped
1/2 tsp Salt
Fresh ground Pepper to taste

Preheat oven to 375F

In a large skillet, heat the oil and stir in all other ingredients. Cook over low heat for 30 minutes or until soft and thick. Remove with slotted spoon into pieshell.

Topping:
5 ripe plum Tomatoes
1 cup black Olives, pitted and sliced
6 cloves Garlic, chopped
10 Anchovy fillets, rinsed and drained
1 tbsp Olive oil
Fresh ground Pepper to taste
1 tbsp Thyme leaves

Halve tomatoes lengthwise. Remove core and seeds. Cut lengthwise again. Arrange in layers in pieshell, alternating with anchovy fillets. Sprinkle olives on top. Combine garlic and oil and sprinkle on top. Sprinkle with pepper and thyme. Bake 30 to 40 minutes or until crust is golden brown and filling is bubbly. Let stand 10 minutes before serving. Serve with a white Zinfandel wine.

South of France Fish Soup

4 c fish Stock
2 tbsp Tomato paste
1 large can plum Tomatoes, peeled and chopped
1/2 tbsp Pernod (or other anise-flavored liqueur)
3 cloves Garlic, minced
1 c fresh Fennel bulb, chopped
Salt and fresh ground Pepper to taste

Combine the stock, tomatoes, tomato paste, liqueur, and garlic in a saucepan and bring to a boil. Reduce heat and simmer uncovered for 30 minutes.

Strain the soup and return the liquid to the saucepan. Stir in the fennel and simmer for 5 minutes until fennel is tender. Season with salt and pepper to taste and serve with croutons.

To make fish stock:
2 tbsp Butter
1 1/2 lb Fish pieces or trimmings
3 c Water
2 c white Wine
1/2 tsp Salt
2 Leeks, washed well and chopped
3 Celery stalks, chopped coarse
3 strips Orange rind
3 strips Lemon rind
3 Bay leaves
2 tsp fresh Basil, chopped
2 tsp fresh Rosemary, chopped
1 tsp Thyme
1 tsp Fennel seeds
1 tbsp all-purpose flour

Melt butter in saucepan and add leeks, fennel, orange and lemon rinds, bay leaves, herbs and spices. Cook on medium low heat for 1 minute.

Add water, wine, fish and salt and bring to a boil. Reduce heat and simmer for 30 minutes. Strain stock and chill.

Midnight Stars

  Most of us these days don't know anything about the natural world around us. Unlike our pioneer forefathers who knew all the trees and plants, all the animal tracks and who could "dead reckon" by the stars, we are sadly bereft of native, natural wisdom. And we're intimidated by it. Yet it's easy to recapture our connection to nature.
  I started watching the stars long before I knew what any of the constellations were. Particularly on cold, clear winter nights. I used to walk along a country road every night at midnight and listen to the different crunching noises the frozen snow would make. My footsteps would echo back from the woods until I would stop, dead still, and listen to the awesome silence. With no other town lights around, I would watch the deep black sky and feel overwhelmed by the millions of points of light whirling in the heavens above. More stars than grains of sand on a beach. Countless stars. Einstein once said, "Not everything that counts can be counted, and not everything that can be counted counts". He could have been talking about stars for all I know.
  When I finally started to study the stars and learn their names, and the names of the constellations, I had a problem. I could never "see", or remember, the constellations as they were outlined in all the backyard astronomy books that I read. But then I realized I didn't have to. The constellations are really arbitrarily defined groups of stars that only *appear* to be related to each other -- named thousands of years ago by Greeks and Romans who are long gone. They named them after what they knew in their lives -- bears, dragons (!), birds, and the gods that they believed lived (literally) in the heavens.
  But this is the twentieth century and we have a new sky to live under. So I started my own constellation naming. When I looked at the winter night sky years ago and saw what looked like a big bowtie, I didn't know it was "really" Orion. And now I don't care, because for me it IS the *Bowtie Constellation*. And as I watched what looked like two mountain peaks circle the

pole star in the summer sky, I didn't know it was Cassiopia. I called them *Cleopatra's Bosom.*

I have a whole catalogue of constellations now. And it's wonderfully comforting to watch "my" stars whirling around the heavens in the same predictability that re-assured the ancient Greeks.

So, come to the Inn in the winter and bundle up. On cold clear Saturday nights we brush the snow off the stone patio, set up a telescope, turn off all the lights and re-discover the stars, again for the first time!

There's something extraordinary and magical that happens as everyone snuggles into deck chairs to star gaze. Voices drop instinctively to hushed whispers. As if we were in hallowed space, and perhaps we are. And muffled giggles and guffaws come from under sleeping bags and quilts as people discover and share their own personal cosmology and humor.

We start by rounding up all the star pattern quilts in the Inn to keep warm in. There's a few because they've always been one of my favorite, traditional quilt themes. Next, everyone receives a pad of paper, a pocket flashlight, and black felt pen. You can make your own star map if you like. Find and name your own constellation(s). Reclaim the night sky. Reclaim your connection to nature. All you have to do is be able to "see" a picture in the "dots" that the stars outline, write it down and know it's position relative to the pole star. Your constellation(s) will circle around the sky during the night, if you stay up late enough, and around the sky during the year as the seasons change. But you can always find it.

Last year someone renamed my Cleopatra's Bosom to Madonna's Bosom -- after all, it's a new generation! Someone else "found" a '57 Chevy. A chemist found a molecular structure in Draco. A gardener thought Sagitarius looked more like a watering can than a teapot.

A psychiatrist would probably have a field day with this -- analyzing all the subliminal transferences and projections we make when we create our own stars. But who cares. When we name something we make it ours. The poets tell us, it's "written in the stars". When we write our own stars, do we write our own destiny as well?

* * *

If you want to have your own Star Naming Party, here are some ideas:

Clear the snow away from whatever area you are using. Dig out all the summer deck chairs. Line each chair with a sleeping bag or quilt to keep the cold from everyone's back. It's really important to keep warm. Sitting outside at night in winter can be unpleasantly cold and dampen the party spirits unless you prepare well in advance. Make sure everyone has a warm hat and mitts to wear. Keep feet warm too.

Provide everyone with a pad of paper to draw on, black felt pens and pocket flashlight. Too much light around will obscure the stars. Turn out as many lights as possible.

Have a telescope or binoculars available if possible. The moon is extraordinary in the winter and if someone has never seen it "up close and personal" it can be a moving experience.

Play star theme music, such as "2001", "Star Wars", "The Night Has a Thousand Eyes", "Moonglow" or any others that you can think of.

Serve lots of warm food, especially if anyone is planning to watch the stars until the Morning Star appears! Make the food simple. Finger-food is best, that can be eaten with mitts on, or by removing mitts only briefly.

Use your discretion on serving alcohol. Alcohol shrinks the capillaries and restricts blood flow so people will feel colder faster when they consume alcohol, which could shorten your party. If you serve alcohol, avoid cold drinks. Serve coffee, or cocoa, "laced" with alcohol, for taste. Or, use artificial extracts, such as rum, for flavor. It's up to you.

Aliske Webb

The Quilt Inn

"Name That Star"

Party Fare

Galileo Punch

3 qt Apple Cider
3 c Orange juice
1/2 c Lemon juice
1/2 c Sugar
10 Cinnamon sticks
1 tbsp whole Cloves
1 tbsp ground Nutmeg

Combine orange and lemon juices, sugar, cinnamon sticks, and nutmeg in large pot. Cook over medium heat until sugar dissolves and mixture is completely blended and hot. Add cider and stir well. Strain liquid into warmed punch bowl before serving.

Copernicus Crudites

1 lb green Beans	) vary quantities
1 Cauliflower head, cut into florets	) depending on
1 Broccoli head, cut into florets	) number of guests
1 lb Carrots, peeled and sliced lengthwise	) approx. 1/2 lb
1 lb Parsnips, peeled and sliced lengthwise	) per person

Steam vegetables in batches until tender but still crisp. Serve in warmed casserole or basket lined with towel to keep them warm.

Dip:
6 oz red Kidney beans
3 Garlic cloves, chopped
1 Jalapeno pepper, cored and seeded

2 tsp Vinegar
1/4 c Water
1/2 c vegetable Oil
1 tsp Paprika
1 tsp fresh ground Pepper
1/4 tsp Chili powder
Dash Hot sauce (Tobasco will do)

Soak beans overnight in cold water.

Drain beans, place in saucepan with new cold water and bring to a boil. Reduce heat and simmer for 45 minutes or until tender. Drain and cool.

Process garlic and jalapeno in blender. Add beans. Continue to process while adding water, vinegar, oil and spices. Blend until smooth.

Line bottom of shallow casserole with bean paste. Cover paste with 1 1/2 c guacamole and set aside.

Topping:
1 1/2 c sour Cream
1/2 c Cheddar cheese, grated
1/2 c plum Tomatoes, seeded and diced fine
1/4 c black Olives, chopped fine
1 tsp Garlic powder
1/4 tsp Chili powder
1/4 tsp ground Cummin
1/2 tsp fresh ground Pepper
Salt to taste

Preheat oven to 425F.

Combine sour cream, garlic and chili powders, cumin, salt and pepper. Blend well and spread on guacamole. Sprinkle with cheese, tomatoes and olives. Bake for 15 minutes.

Aliske Webb

Hubble's Heavenly Hot Chocolate

For each person served:
- melt 3 ounces of a good quality chocolate candy bar in top of double boiler
- whisk in 1 cup milk
- bring just to boil and whisk in
- 1 beaten egg yolk
- heat thoroughly and serve

What's My Wine?

It's been a beautiful Summer here at the Inn. This afternoon I was lazing on the verandah reflecting on the abundance of joy and happiness that we have shared with our guests, friends and general well-wishers, when, much to my delight, I spied an ancient Citroen huffing its way up the driveway. The banging of steel on steel accompanied by noxious exhaust fumes announced the arrival of our local grape-grower and vintner, Pierre LaBouche, of Labouche Freres Winery. What a delight to see him!

Pierre brought our order of wine. If you find the Inn out of your chosen dinner wine blame it on the vagaries of Pierre's visits. He turns up whenever the spirit(s) move him.

We carried cases of wine to the cellar where Pierre made his routine inspection of our wine cellar. We've never made it past a "B-minus" in his rating -- perhaps because we don't stock enough of his wines!

The wine cellar was never intended as such. In fact the cellar is only under part of the house, and is really only a root cellar dug under one side of the Inn. Perhaps it was an afterthought. The rough dirt walls and massive wood ceiling beams make it an ideal wine cellar, though, with only the addition of some simple racks.

After opening and sampling a robust red wine ("From the cellars directly to you, *mon ami*," Pierre said), Pierre asked if I would like to play a little parlor game with him. "Let's test your knowledge of wine trivia, my budding *sommelier*," he said. "And perhaps the guests of the beautiful Quilt Inn, and readers of your upcoming cookbook, will benefit from this knowledge."

I readily agreed, but not before fortifying myself with some more red. "Let the game begin!" I said.

1. True or false? Wines made from grapes have to be aged whereas wines made from raisins do not.

False. In Italy, vintners dry the harvested grapes until they are raisin-like to make Vin Santo or Recioto della Amarone. These wines need aging just as wines from freshly picked grapes do.

2. Is red wine more fattening than white?

I was prepared to put down my now almost empty glass, but Pierre hastened to assure me that the calorie content of a wine depends on its alcohol and residual sugar. A California Chardonnay, for example, at 12.5% alcohol will have more calories than a Beaujolais at 11% alcohol. Well, Pierre, perhaps just a touch more--not as fattening, you know.

3. Michael's birthday arrives soon...how do you open Champagne to avoid the pop and a fountain?

Hold the cork firmly and gently twist the bottle away from the cork. The cork should not move. "Here, I'll show you," Pierre said, having retrieved a bottle of Moet from the Inn's racks. Sure enough, when opened the way he suggested, no pop, no foam, just a light expression of air, like the sigh you make after tasting your first sip. Which we did.

4. Are all pink wines sweet?

No. Many pink wines, such as rose, are dry, especially those from the Rhone Valley, such as Tavel and Lirac.

5. The vintage date on a bottle of wine tells you: (a) the birth year of the winemaker's first child (b) the winemaker's wedding anniversary, so he won't forget (c) the year the grapes were picked and crushed (d) the year the bottle was made (e) the year the wine was bottled

The answer is (c), although (b) would not be a bad idea!

6. How should you hold a wine glass?

Oh, oh. I could hear another demonstration coming from Pierre, and of course the glasses needed to be refilled. "It's just educational, *mon ami*," he said with a glow *(it might have been the champagne)*. "Hold a wine glass by the stem or the base, not by the bowl. Otherwise you will warm up a chilled white, or cover up the bouquet of a red."

7. True or false? Fill your wine glasses as full as possible, not only to show your generosity, but to give a better appreciation of the color of the wine.

False. A wine glass should only be filled to the two-thirds level, to allow you to swirl the wine to produce a concentrated bouquet. *(Also, if the glass is too full, your nose will get wet: I think Jimmy Durante started this tradition.)*

8. Pierre swore on his mother's grave that if you sucked a warm Sauterne through a straw (Sauterne is the sweet white dessert wine from Bordeaux) you could cure your hiccups. True or false?

Absolutely false. *(But if you suck enough wine this way you won't care if you have hiccups or not!)* And, Pierre's mother is still alive, too!

9. Are dry wines with a sugar count of zero really dry?

No wine is completely dry. There will always be some unfermented sugar in it.

10. True or false: Alsace is a German wine region.

Well, this question started Pierre and I reminiscing about "The Rocky and Bullwinkle Show", (thereby disclosing our ages) -- when "our heroes" attempted to save the French wine-growing region of "Applesauce Lorraine", so it took awhile to come back to the question. (Boris: "I hate Moose!" Natasha: "I know you do, dollink!")

In any event, for those of you who are still with us, the answer is false. Alsace is a wine region in northeastern France, bordering on Germany's Baden region. It's distinctive green, long-necked bottles resemble those of the German Mosel wines.

11. True or false: Champagne glasses should be placed wet into

the freezer, to frost them so that the wine will remain as cold as possible.

Oh oh, again. Another Champagne question. Sure enough, out came another bottle, accompanied by frosted glasses. What happened? The wetness kills the bubbles and makes the Champagne go flat.

Which brought us to a discussion of the shape a champagne glass should be. Pierre asserted that Hollywood movies aside, champagne should always be served in a tall slim fluted glass -- in order to preserve the bubbles. *Mon dieu*, whoever started serving champagne in those flat-bowled stem glasses should be flogged, he tells me. The flat bowl lets the bubbles out faster, which explains why the champagne served at most wedding receptions is flat by the time it's served to you.

(The tipsiest I remember ever being happened one New Year's Eve, drinking champagne floats -- vanilla ice cream and champagne. If you think cola fizzes when it hits ice cream, wait until you see champagne fizz!)

Back to the quiz: *(albeit unsteadily)*

12. How do you pronounce Riesling?

Well, I think it has to do with how much you have consumed, but the correct answer is to say Reez-ling.

13. True or false: the longer the cork, the more expensive the wine?

Strangely, true. Long corks are more expensive and are of better quality.

14. Vinho Verde is:
(a) the color of paint that your wife wants matched exactly at the True Value (b) a greeting used in Spanish wine bars (c) one of the Canary Islands (d) any Portuguese wine made from green grapes (e) a light zingy white wine grown in the Minho region of Portugal (f) the color of your Dad's '53 Nash Rambler.

The answer is (e), although (f) is probably true, too.

15. What is a Buzbag? (a) slang for too many wine samplings with good friends (b) a Spanish wine skin (c) a Turkish wine made from Okuzgozu grapes (d) a parasite that attacks vine roots.

The answer is (c). No other comments, please!

16. What are wine diamonds?

Not, as one might expect, a *Michelin Guide* rating at a restaurant, but rather potassium bitartrate crystals that precipitate in a wine that has been chilled too quickly. They are harmless, tasteless, and odorless, and in fact are a sign of quality. They show the wine has not been pasteurized and cold-stabilized, as are less expensive table wines.

* * *

You can stay at a country inn for your health -- or you can stay at an inn to get away from your healthy regime once in a while. Here are some special occasion recipes with extra spirit! Let's tell it like it is: none of them are good for you. Which is why we are starting with dessert first, but as Oscar Wilde said, "The only way to get rid of temptation is to yield to it".

Amaretto Cheesecake

Crust:
1 c Graham cracker crumbs
1/2 c toasted Almonds, chopped fine
2 tbsp Sugar
1/4 c melted Butter

Preheat oven to 450F.

Mix ingredients and press into bottom of 9-inch pan. Set aside.

Filling:
4 pkgs Cream cheese (250 g each)
1 c Sugar
3 tbsp Flour
4 Eggs
1 c sour cream
1/4 c Amaretto Di Saronno

Combine cream cheese, sugar and flour, mixing well until blended. Add eggs, one at a time, mixing until combined. Blend in sour cream and Amaretto.

Pour over crust. Bake for 10 minutes. Reduce heat to 250F and bake 1 hour. Remove from oven, cool on wire rack. Chill.

Glaze:
1/2 c Apricot jam
1 tbsp Amaretto Di Saronno

Combine jam and liqueur in saucepan. Heat until warm and smooth. Strain mixture and pour over cheesecake before serving. Garnish with toasted flaked almonds.

Creme Brulee

1 can undiluted Condensed Milk
3/4 c fresh brewed Coffee
1/4 c Cognac
2/3 c Sugar
1 tsp Vanilla extract
1/8 tsp Salt
4 Eggs
1/4 c brown Sugar
Preheat oven to 350F

Combine milk, cognac and coffee in saucepan. Heat until bubbles form around edge. Add granulated sugar, vanilla and salt, stirring until sugar dissolves. Beat eggs well in mixing bowl. Gradually stir in hot milk mixture into eggs. Pour into 4 cup souffle dish or ovenproof casserole, or individual ramekins.

Quilt Inn Country Cookbook

Place dish(es) in pan of hot water and bake for 50-60 minutes or until center is set and knifetip inserted in center comes out clean. Chill until cool.

To serve: sprinkle brown sugar over custard. Place as close as possible under preheated broiler and broil until sugar melts and browns.

Raspberries In Love Sauce

2 c fresh Raspberries *(frozen will do)*
1/2 c confectioners' Sugar
1 tbsp fresh Lemon juice
1/4 c Amaretto di Saronna

Puree raspberries in blender. Add sugar, lemon juice and amaretto. Process until smooth. Strain to remove seeds if desired. Pour over sponge cake, ice cream, or any other would-be plain and plebian dessert.

Grand Marinier Sauce

1/3 c Grand Marnier *(or Cointreau)*
1 c whipping Cream
3/4 c Sugar
5 Egg yolks
1 tbsp Sugar

Beat egg yolks in double boiler until light and frothy. Beat in sugar and place of simmering water for 20 minutes, stirring constantly, until thickened. Remove from heat and continue beating until cool. Stir in Grand Marnier and chill.

Whip cream until it begins to thicken. Add 1 tablespoon sugar and beat until thick but pourable. Fold in egg mixture and chill until ready to serve.

Keep both of these sauces made up in advance in the refrigerator for last minute out-of-the-hat dessert miracles!

Drunkard's Path Turkey

Our friend Gail makes it through the one meal of the year that she cooks this way: she gets up at ten o'clock (her children are grown-ups, or pretend to be); she does her face and hair and sets out for the kitchen; she opens a bottle of her favorite wine and sips it while she makes Christmas dinner. By the time the turkey is cooked, so is Gail! This isn't her recipe, but it reminds us of her.

1 Turkey, cut in pieces

Marinade:
1 c dry Red Wine
1/2 c Bourbon
1/2 c dry Sherry
1/3 Soya sauce
3 tbsp Oil
2 tbsp Sugar
5 whole Anise seeds
1 tbsp fresh Ginger, minced
Fresh ground Pepper to taste

Mix all the marinade ingredients in large bowl. Add turkey pieces and coat thoroughly. Cover and let sit for 3 hours.

Preheat oven to 325F.

Remove turkey from marinade and place in roasting pan. Pour 1/2 c of marinade over turkey. Bake 1 hour, turning and basting as necessary. Increase oven heat to 450F.

Glaze:
1 c Bourbon
2/3 c Honey
2/3 c Ketchup
1/4 c brown Sugar

Mix glaze ingredients thoroughly in bowl. Brush turkey with glaze. Bake 30 minutes, basting and turning every 5 minutes.

Quilt Inn Country Cookbook

    Here's a little wine-related trivia for you: some of you may remember the 1950's game show "The $64000 Question". If you do, you may even remember that the first contestant to achieve the top level (at each level you risked your previous earnings for a chance at double-or-nothing) was a Marine captain named Richard McCutcheon. This was before the "fix was in", and his category of specialization was, surprisingly, not military history, but cooking. With an audience estimated a 55 million watching, on September 13, 1955, he became the first to scale game show Everest.
    For $64000, he was asked to name the five dishes and two wines from the menu served by King George VI of England for French President Albert Lebrun in 1939. He did: consomme quenelles, filet de truite saumonee, petits pois a la francaises, sauce maltaise and corbeille. The wines were Chateau d'Yquem and Madera Sercal. I guess knowing that trivia is worth $64,000....

My Dear Madeira Spinach

4 lb fresh Spinach
1/2 lb fresh Mushrooms, sliced
1/2 c Cream
1/4 c Water
1/4 c Madeira wine
3 tbsp Butter
1/4 tsp Nutmeg
Salt and fresh ground Pepper to taste

Steam spinach until soft. Drain thoroughly, pat dry with paper towels. Process in blender for 1 minute, or chop fine. Drain liquid again. Add butter, nutmeg, salt, pepper and cream. Set aside, but keep warm.

Saute mushrooms lightly. Add to spinach mixture. Stir in Madeira. Reheat and serve.

Aliske Webb

Madeira Soup

2 1/2 c chicken Stock
2 1/2 c beef Stock
1/2 c Madeira
4 Leeks, washed and chopped
1 Onion, chopped
3 tbsp Butter
3 tbsp all-purpose Flour
1 lb fresh Mushrooms, chopped
Salt and fresh ground Pepper to taste

Melt butter in saucepan and add leeks and onions. Cook on medium low heat for 10 minutes or until tender. Sprinkle with flour and cook another 5 minutes. Add remaining ingredients and bring just to a boil. Reduce heat and simmer, uncovered, for 30 minutes or until mushrooms are soft.

Place in blender and puree until smooth. Return to pot and heat thoroughly before serving. Garnish with chopped chives.

Hot Wine Sauce

1/2 c Port wine
1/2 c red Currant jelly
Juice of 1/2 Lemon
3 whole Cloves
1 tbsp Butter
1 tbsp Cornstarch
Dash Cayenne pepper

Combine all ingredients, except port and cornstarch, in saucepan and simmer for 5 minutes. If desired, strain sauce. Add Port and stir 3 or 4 tablespoons of the hot liquid into the cornstarch to form paste; gradually add paste back to hot liquid, stirring contantly, to thicken.

The Orchard

Workmen arrived this morning and started cutting down trees in the orchard. The orchard is over a hundred years old and is surrounded on three sides by a neat stone wall. The wall is three feet high and a foot and a half wide. It is completely free-standing and made without mortar, yet all the stones fit neatly into place. The wall was made by an itinerant stonemason who travelled around the county building walls to pay for his supper.

This spring, we are losing seven trees to old age and blight. They are all along the east wall which is the oldest part of the orchard. It's hard to lose one tree, much less seven. They are like grandparents, or old members of the community. They were here before we arrived, and we assumed they would be here forever.

Sometimes, I guess, we ignore their steadfastness until it is threatened, or gone. But we looked after our trees. Why us. Why are they gone. It feels like ponderous mortality. Seems like the tree just reaches full productive maturity and then it is gone. Like people. We work and grow and learn all we can to become productive mature members of our community, then we, too, are gone and others take our place.

Tree sentimentality seems to be an attitude I brought from a city childhood. Perhaps because in the city there are so few trees, and we are so removed from them and green, growing life. We long for trees like missing relatives and desperately hold on to the pathetic concrete shrouded survivors on downtown streets.

Here in the country where trees and green life abound there is a different perspective. Rather than a maudlin sentimentality, there is a simple respect for life, and its ebb and flowing nature. In the nursery, saplings are thinned to make room for healthy full size plants. Not every plant will survive, if they all try to. A fruit tree must be pruned to make healthier growth next year. In the orchard, an old diseased tree is removed so it doesn't infect the others. In the light and space it leaves, a new young and vigorous tree is planted, ensuring another generation will grow up and continue to be a productive orchard.

And the remaining old trees shade the young trees from the heat of summer and the cold winds of winter until they are strong enough to stand alone. The myriad leaves fall and rot and refertilize the ground the saplings will grow in. That's the nature of the orchard. We are all part of that reassuring cycle of nature.

President John Kennedy was conferring with his gardener about a new tree that was to be planted. Wanting to produce quicker results for the President, the gardener explained to Kennedy that the species of tree he had chosen was a very slow growing variety that would not reach maturity for almost one hundred years; perhaps he would like to choose another. But Kennedy's inimitable answer was, "Then we have no time to lose; the tree must be planted today"!

Michael and I were going to drive into Clareville tomorrow, to Johnson's Nursery. But I think we'll go this afternoon instead.

* * *

We often think of orchard fruits, like peaches, only as dessert fare. But these versatile peaches can be delicious ingredients in entire meals, from aperitif to dessert. Here are some unusual, peachy dishes.

Aldous Huxley wrote: "Champagne has the taste of an apple peeled with a steel knife."

However, Brillat-Savarin said: "Burgundy makes you think of silly things, Bordeaux makes you talk about them, and Champagne makes you do them!"

Peach Cocktail

Place a slice of fresh Peach in bottom of champagne flute. Splash in peach schnapps and fill with chilled champagne. Sit n' sip.

Peach Antipasto

Juice of fresh Lime
1/2 lb Prosciutto ham, sliced thin
4 ripe Peaches

Peel and pit peaches, cut into slices.

Toss with lime juice. Serve on individual dishes, alternating slices of ham and peach, garnish with parsley.

Peach Blue Cheese Salad

3 ripe Peaches
3 oz Blue Cheese*
1/4 c toasted Walnuts, chopped
1/3 c fresh Lime juice
1/4 c Walnut Oil
2 tsp white wine Vinegar
1/2 tsp Dijon Mustard
Salt and fresh ground Pepper to taste
Bunch Watercress or shredded lettuce

Whisk lime juice, oil, vinegar, mustard, salt and pepper together in bowl. Peel, pit and slice peaches. Add to dressing, toss to coat. Marinate 1 hour.

Arrange watercress or lettuce bed on serving platter or individual plates. Place peach slices on top, drizzle remaining dressing. Crumble cheese over peaches and sprinkle with walnuts. Serve chilled.

* There are many wonderful blue cheeses on the market these days. Try different ones until you find the one to your taste, and to suit the purpose. Although they all have a distinctive strong flavor, I find French and German blues, such as Bleu de Bresse, to be milder, creamier and more spreadable; English Stilton is milder and crumbly; Danish bleu is the saltiest and moderately crumbly. And of course, you can never go wrong with Italy's Gorgonzola.

Peach Salsa

3 Peaches, pitted and diced
1 tbsp fresh Lime juice
1/4 c sweet red Pepper, diced
1 green Onion, chopped fine
4 tsp fresh Coriander, chopped fine
1 tbsp jalapeno Pepper, minced
2 tsp brown Sugar
1 tsp Vinegar
Salt and fresh ground Pepper to taste

Peel, pit and dice peaches and toss with lime juice in bowl. Add red pepper, green onion, coriander and jalapeno. Stir sugar, vinegar, salt and pepper together until sugar is dissolved. Pour over peach mixture and toss. Serve with nachos.

Peach Chutney

25 large ripe Peaches, peeled, pitted and diced
6 c Sugar
4 c cider Vinegar
3 tbsp preserved Ginger, chopped
3/4 c candied Citron, chopped
1/4 c candied Lemon, chopped
3 Cinnamon sticks
30 whole Cloves
3/4 tsp Coriander seed

Prepare fruit and mix with ginger, citron and lemon peel.

Tie cinnamon, cloves and coriander in cloth bag.

Make a syrup of the sugar and vinegar. Bring syrup to a boil. Add fruit and spice bag. Simmer for 10 minutes. Remove spice bag. Pour into sterilized jars and seal.

Tender Peach Tenderloins

1 1/2 lb pork tenderloins
4 fresh Peaches, peeled, pitted and halved
1 c dry white Wine
1 c Orange juice
3 tbsp soy sauce
1/4 c fresh Basil, chopped
2 tsp fresh Ginger, minced
2 tsp brown Sugar

Stir together wine, orange juice, soy sauce, basil and ginger. Add pork, turning to coat, cover and marinate 1 hour, turning occasionally. Reserve marinade.

Transfer pork to grill and sear for 2 minutes each side. Cover grill and lower heat (or raise grill). Cook 15 minutes, basting several times with marinade. Turn and cook thoroughly. Let stand 10 minutes covered with foil before carving.

Brush peach halves with marinade and 10 minutes before tenderloin is cooked, place on cooler part of grill. Baste 2 or 3 times and turn once. Bring remaining marinade to boil. Reduce heat, simmer until slightly thickened. Add brown sugar, simmer 5 minutes. Use as hot sauce with pork.

To serve, place pork on bed of greens and garnish with peach halves.

Peach Pie

1 Pie crust
1 lb Peaches, peeled and sliced
1 Egg
2 tbsp Flour
1/2 c Sugar
1/3 c melted Butter

Preheat oven to 400F.

Place peach slices in layers around pie crust.

Combine egg, flour, butter and sugar. Pour mixture over peaches. Bake for 15 minutes at 400F, then reduce to 300F and bake 50 minutes. Serve hot or cold. Garnish with whipped cream and fresh peach slice.

Stuffed Peaches

6 Freestone Peaches, peeled, pitted and halved
2 c mixed Berries (raspberry, blackberries, red currants)
1/4 c Sugar
1/4 c Raisins
2 tbsp Walnuts, chopped
1 tbsp Lemon juice
1/2 c Corn syrup
Cinnamon

Preheat oven to 350F.

Mix berries, raisins, walnuts, sugar and lemon juice. Fill peach half with berry mixture. Place each peach half in large muffin pan to keep from rolling over, or in shallow baking dish. Pour corn syrup over peaches. Bake for 1 hour.

Remove from oven. Dust with granulated sugar and cinnamon. Place under broiler until golden brown. Serve immediately.

Canned Laughter

Once a month a TV camera crew arrives at the Inn, accompanied by "Aunts" Ivy and Millie, who are local celebs on the KORN-TV station. They like to use our library to can (tape) some of their TV programs. The library has wide-plank wood floors, tartan-patterned wallpaper and one whole wall of book shelves. Over the small fireplace are framed eighteenth century hunting scenes. There's a leather sofa and plaid wingback chairs with good reading lights that are comfortable enough to invite you to curl up with a good book, but straight enough to keep you from falling asleep. It's a very masculine-looking, "lord of the manor" sort of room which makes it an interesting backdrop for these two grey haired ladies' "fireside chats".

Aunt Millie and Aunt Ivy are good friends who have agreed to disagree about almost everything. If one likes hot weather, the other prefers cold. If one votes liberal, the other votes conservative. If one is logical, the other is chaotic. If there are two sides to anything, these two will find them. And they've made a name for themselves locally by playing point-counterpoint on their program.

"Canning" TV shows always reminds me of my Grama and the crock of pickles she inevitably had aging in the "summer kitchen" out back, and the jars of jams and relishes that were lined up on an old hutch.

Michael and I both grew up in a climate that had short summers, followed by what seemed to be an interminably cold and snowy winter. Therefore, the growing season was short, and the depths of January were always brightened by savoring the fruits and vegetables which had been carefully nurtured in late June, July and early August. So, we don't mind the heat when it comes. We like to say that we are storing it up for the Winter, the better to melt the snowdrifts that stood between us and our dormant garden.

Here at The Quilt Inn, the seasonal swing is not as pronounced, but it still calls for "putting up" fruits and vegetables, the better to remember the Summer growing season.

There are other reasons as well. What you prepare at home and serve has less salt and sugar, and relies more on the natural tastes and textures than does "store bought". The natural flavors, especially of jams and sweet preserves, are usually more satisfying, so a little often goes a long way.

At The Quilt Inn, in the orchard, you see peach, plum and pear trees, a single nectarine and apricot. There is also a farm garden, which produces abundant quantities of beans, cucumbers, tomatoes, fresh herbs, the ubiquitous zucchini, and more.

Here are some of our favorite "canned sunshine" recipes.

* * *

Michael's Fuzzy Navel Jam

5 c prepared ripe Peaches
2 tbsp Lemon juice
2 tbsp grated Orange rind
3 kl/2 c Sugar
1 box Certo fruit pectin
1/8 tsp Butter
1/4 c Peach Schnapps

Peel and pit peaches. Grind or finely chop. Place 5 cups prepared fruit in saucepan. Add lemon juice and orange rind. Mix pectin crystal with 1/4 cup of the sugar. Blend well. Slowly add fruit pectin mixture to prepared fruit in saucepan.

Place over high heat and stir constantly until mixture comes to a boil. Add remaining sugar. Continue to stire and boil hard for 1 minute. Mixture should thicken. Remove from heat, stir in peach schnapps. Skim off foam. Pour into sterilized jars and cover with new lids. Store opened jam in refrigerator.

Aunt Ivy's Peach Chutney

4 lb freestone Peaches, peeled and chopped
1 c seedless Raisins
2 cloves Garlic, minced
3/4 c chopped Onion
1/3 c drained chopped Ginger
1 tbsp Chili powder
1 tbsp Mustard seed
1 tsp Salt
4 tbsp mixed Pickling Spice
2 1/2 c cider Vinegar
1 1/2 lb Brown Sugar

Tie pickling spice in cheesecloth bag. Place in large bowl or crock with all other ingredients. Cover, let stand 24 hours.

Turn mixture into heavy kettle, bring to boil and simmer uncovered for 45 minutes or until chutney is thick, stirring occasionally. Remove spice bag. Ladle mixture into sterilized jars and seal. Store in cool, dark place.

Strawberry Daiqairi Jam

1 c prepared ripe strawberries
2/3 c unsweetened Pineapple juice
1/3 c Lime juice
3 c Sugar
1 pouch Certo liquid fruit pectin
4 tbsp dark rum

Clean and hull strawberries. Crush berries. Place 1 cup berries into non-metal bowl. Add pineapple, lime and sugar. Bring mixture to a full boil for 1 minute. Add liquid fruit pectin and rum. Stir and skim for 5 minutes. Let cool slightly to prevent fruit from floating to top. Pour into sterilized jars. Cover with new lids or hot paraffin.

Peach Relish

2 c finely chopped fresh Peaches
3 3/4 c sugar
1/2 c white vinegar
2 tbsp dry Mustard
2 tbsp Onion, grated
1 pouch Certo liquid fruit pectin

Combine fruit, sugar, vinegar, mustard and onion in large saucepan. Cook and stir over high heat until mixture comes to boil. Boil hard for 1 minute, stirring constantly. Remove from heat. Stir in liquid pectin. Skim off foam. Stir and skim for 5 minutes while cooling slightly. Pour into sterilized jars, seal with new lids or hot paraffin.

Sweet Georgia Jam

5 lb Peaches
1/4 c Lemon juice
1 c pure Maple syrup
2 tsp Cinnamon

Blanch peaches in boiling water to loosen skins. Drain, cool and peel. Pit and chop finely.

Combine peaches, lemon juice, maple syrup and cinnamon in non-aluminium pot. Bring to a boil and gently cook for 10 minutes or until thick. Test by dropping onto cool plate -- jam should hold its shape if it's cooked.

Remove from heat. Skim off any foam. Ladle into sterilized jars and seal. This is delicious served with pancakes or crepes.

Quilt Inn Country Cookbook

Easy Anyberry Jam

The great thing about this jam is that it tastes different every time depending on the quantities of different berries you have on hand, so from one recipe comes several flavors...

4 qt fresh Raspberries, Blackberries, Strawberries (or any combination)
3 Apples, tart and finely chopped
1 c Honey
2 tbsp Lemon juice

Crush some of the berries in a large kettle. Add remaining berries and other ingredients. Bring to a boil and continue boiling for 30 minutes or until mixture thickens, stirring frequently. Remove from heat; skim off any foam. Pour into sterilized jars and seal.

Apricot Brandy Conserve

2 1/1 c Apricots, pitted and chopped
2 tbsp Lemon juice
3 1/2 c Sugar
1/2 box Certo Fruit Pectin
1/4 c Brandy

Pit but do not peel apricots. Add lemon juice. Mix fruit with pectin in saucepan. Bring to boil. Stir in sugar and continue boiling for 30 minutes. Skim off any foam. Stir in brandy. Remove from heat; stir and skim for 5 minutes as jam cools. Pour into sterilized jars and seal.

Strawberries in Love

5 1/2 c Strawberries, washed and hulled
4 c Sugar
1/4 c Lemon juice
1 pouch Certo fruit pectin (1/2 bottle)
2/3 c Amaretto di Saronna liqueur

Wash berries and mix with sugar and lemon juice in large kettle. Bring to a boil; stir in pectin. Continue boiling for 25-30 minutes. Test for setting by dropping onto cool plate - jam should keep its shape if cooked. Remove from heat; skim foam from top and stir while cooling to prevent fruit from floating to surface. Stir in liqueur. Pour into sterilized jars and seal.

Savory Jelly

This is excellent served with turkey or baked ham.

2 c dry white Wine
3 c Sugar
2 tbsp Tarragon flavored Vinegar
2 tsp dried Tarragon leaves, chopped fine
1 pouch Certo liquid pectin (1/2 bottle)

Combine wine, sugar and vinegar in saucepan. Add tarragon leaves. Bring to full boil and boil for 1 minute, stirring constantly. Remove from heat. Stir in pectin. Strain mixture through fine sieve to remove leaves, if desired. Pour into sterilized jars and seal.

Songs from the Hearth

I have a copy of *The Woman's Exchange Cook Book* by Mrs. Minnie Palmer, published in 1901 by the W.B. Conkey Company of Chicago. It's been in our family a long time. I think it was my great grandmother's.

Now, before you think it is valuable or something, let me tell you this is a very beaten up copy. In fact, the original cover was lost years ago, as as long as I can remember it's been held together by the very beaten up cover of another (lost) book called, "Heart Songs" which as a little girl I misread the title, and always thought it said Hearth Songs. Somehow that seemed appropriate to call it -- a cookbook *would* contain songs from the hearth -- isn't that what Shakespeare was alluding to when he wrote: "If music be the food of love..."

Unlike Elena Molokhovets' book about pre-Revolutionary Russian aristocratic excesses, Mrs. Palmer's book is a plain, down-to-earth anthology of everything a North American homemaker at the turn of the century needed to know. It includes everything from dressing game, to preserving food, to baking pies and making ice cream delicacies.

For extra value in the 500-odd pages, there are chapters on cooking for an invalid, how to run a nursery, the laundry (how to make soap), how to make perfumes and cosmetics, and, remedies for common ailments, which is my favourite.

So, before we become too nostalgic about the good old days, here are some of the *invaluable* cures you might want to try...

To Stop Bleeding

Apply wet tea leaves, or scrapings of sole leather (!) to a fresh cut and it will stop bleeding, or apply a paste of flour and vinegar.

To Stop Bleeding at the Nose

Bathe the feet in very hot water, drinking at the same time a pint of cayenne pepper tea, or hold both hands above the head.

Tootheache

The worst toothache, or neuralgia coming from the teeth, may be speedily and delightfully ended by the application of a bit of clean cotton saturated in the solution of ammonia to the defective tooth. Sometimes the late sufferer is prompted to momentary laughter by the application, but the pain will disappear. *(Try suggesting this to your dentist!)*

Relief from Asthma

Sufferers from asthma should get a muskrat skin and wear it over their lungs with the fur side next to the body. Or, soak blotting paper in saltpeter water, then dry, burning at night in the patient's bedroom.

Earache

Take a bit of cotton batting, put upon it a pinch of black pepper gather it up and tie it, dip in sweet oil and insert into the heat; put a flannel bandage over the head to keep it warm. It will give immediate relief.

And finally, Cough Syrup

Syrup of squills 4 ounces, syrup of tolu 4 ounces, tincture of bloodroot one and one half ounces, camphorated tincture of opium 4 ounces. Mix. *(I wonder where you find squills these days...)*

* * *

When I think of a hearth I always think of the smell of warm loaves of bread baking...

Country Inn Brown Oat Bread

4 1/2 c all-purpose Flour
1 1/2 c rolled Oats
2 c boiling Water
3/4 c Molasses
1 tsp Sugar
2 tsp Salt
1 tbsp Shortening
1 package granulated Yeast
1/2 warm Water

Preheat oven to 350F and lightly grease two loaf pans.

Stir oats and salt into boiling water. Add shortening. Combine yeast, sugar and warm water. Let stand 10 minutes. Add molasses to oatmeal mixture, then enough flour to make stiff dough. Add yeast mixture and mix well. Let rise until light and double in size. Punch down and split into two loaf pans. Let rise again. Bake for 45 minutes. Remove from oven and brush with butter. Cook on wire rack.

Fresh Herb Bread

2 1/2 c all-purpose Flour
1 c Cottage cheese, creamed
1 Egg, beaten
2 tbsp Sugar
1/4 c warm Water
1 tbsp Onion, minced fine
2 tsp Caraway seeds (or try Dill, or Rosemary)
1 tsp Salt
1/4 tsp Soda
1 tbsp Butter
1 package granulated Yeast

Preheat oven to 350F and lightly grease an ovenproof casserole dish.

Heat cottage cheese in saucepan to lukewarm. Soften yeast in warm water. In large mixing bowl, combine in order cheese, sugar, onion, butter, caraway, salt, soda, egg and softened yeast. Add enough flour to make stiff dough. Cover and let rise until double in size. Punch down and turn into casserole. Let rise again and bake for 40 minutes or until golden brown. Remove from oven, brush with butter and serve warm.

Fresh Herb Soda Bread

2 c whole wheat Flour
2 c all-purpose Flour
2 c Buttermilk
2 tsp Sugar
1 tsp baking Soda
1 tsp baking Powder
1 tbsp Salt
3 tbsp Butter
1/2 tsp Sage
1/2 tsp Basil
1/2 tsp Thyme
1/2 tsp Chives
1/2 tsp Marjoram

Preheat oven to 375F and lightly grease a baking sheet.

Sift dry ingredients together in large mixing bowl. Cut in butter until mixture forms crumbles. Stir in herbs. Stir in buttermilk and form dough into ball. Knead dough lightly on floured surface until smooth. Transfer to baking sheet and form into rough loaf. Bake for 40 minutes or until loaf sounds hollow when tapped. Cool on wire rack and serve warm.

English Ale Bread

3 cups self-rising Flour
1/4 c Sugar
12 oz strong English Ale *(that's beer)*
1 tsp grated Orange rind

Preheat oven to 350F and lightly grease loaf pan.

Mix flour and sugar thoroughly. Add orange rind. Stir in ale until batter is formed. Place in loaf pan and bake for 1 hour or until golden brown.

Greek Braid Bread

3 1/2 c sifted Flour
3 tbsp Sugar
2 Eggs, beaten
3/4 c Milk, at room temperature
1/4 c warm Water
1/4 c Butter, softened
1/4 tsp Salt
1 package dry Yeast
Sesame seeds for topping (optional)

Preheat oven to 350F well in advance of baking, and lightly grease baking sheet.

Dissolve yeast in warm water and 1 teaspoon of the sugar in large mixing bowl. Set aside for 15 minutes. Yeast mixture should triple in size.

Heat milk in saucepan but do not boil. Dissolve remaining sugar and salt in milk. Add butter. Blend thoroughly. Stir milk mixture into yeast. Add half the beaten egg and blend well. Add dough until stiff dough formed. Mix with hands and knead thoroughly. Form into ball and place in bowl. Set in warm place for 1 hour or until dough doubles in size.

Punch down and roll to 1/2 inch thickness. Cut into 1 inch strips. Take 3 strips and pinch ends together. Braid strips and pinch ends together. For variation, form into ring by bringing both pinched ends together and tucking together.

Place on baking sheet, leaving room between loaves for expansion. Cover with tea towel and set in warm place to rise. Loaves should double in size. Brush gently with remaining beaten egg. Sprinkle with sesame seeds. Bake for 25 minutes or until golden brown.

Always cool bread completely on wire racks before storing.

Catcher in the Rye Bread

2 c all-purpose Flour
1 c Rye flour
2 tbsp Cornmeal
1 tbsp Caraway seeds
1/4 tsp Sugar
1 tsp Salt
3/4 c warm Water
2 tbsp warm Water
1 Egg
2 tbsp vegetable Oil
1 tbsp Honey
1 package dry Yeast
Fresh ground Pepper to taste

Preheat oven to 375F and lightly grease baking sheet or loaf pan.

Combine yeast, 3/4 cup warm water and sugar in small bowl. Set aside for 10 minutes.

Combine flours, caraway seeds, and salt in large mixing bowl. Add yeast mixture, oil, honey and 2 tablespoons warm water. Mix thoroughly until dough forms. Place on floured surface and knead dough for 10 minutes or until it is smooth and elastic. Form into ball

Lightly oil clean mixing bowl and roll dough ball in bowl to coat with oil. Cover and let dough rise for 1 hour or until double in size. Punch down. Form ball again and let rise again.
Foam loaf and place on baking sheet or in loaf pan. Beat egg with 1 tablespoon of water. Brush loaf with egg mixture.
Sprinkle with caraway seeds and pepper, if desired. Bake for 35 minutes or until golden brown and loaf sounds hollow when tapped lightly.

Graham Bread

4 c Graham flour
2 c all-purpose Flour
4 tsp Baking soda
4 c Buttermilk
1 c Sugar
1 tsp Salt

Preheat oven to 350F and lightly grease 2 loaf pans.

Mix buttermilk and soda until frothy. Combine dry ingredients and add to buttermilk mixture. Pour into loaf pan and bake for 1 hour or until golden brown. Cool on wire rack before storing.

Egg Bread

6 c all-purpose Flour
2 pkg dry Yeast
1 1/2 c Milk
1/3 c Butter
1/2 c Sugar
1 tsp Salt
3 Eggs
1 Egg yolk, beaten lightly
Sesame seeds

Preheat oven to 375F and lightly grease baking sheet to hold 3 loaves.

Sift together 2 cups of flour with yeast. In a saucepan heat milk, butter, sugar and salt until warm. Mix 3 eggs into dry ingredients and beat at low speed for 1 minute, then at high speed for 3 more minutes. Beat in milk mixture. Stir in as much flour by hand as possible.

Turn onto floured surface and knead in enough flour to make a smooth and elastic dough. Shape into 3 balls and place in greased bowl. Cover and let rise for 1 1/2 hours or until dough doubles in size. Punch down, cover and let rest for 15 minutes. Divide dough into 3 portions. Divide each portion into 3 ropes. Pinch together ends of 3 ropes and braid, pinching other ends together. Place each loaf on baking sheet.

Cover and let rise until double again (45 minutes). Combine egg yolk and 1 tablespoon water. Brush on loaves. Sprinkle with sesame seeds and bake for 25 minutes or until golden brown.

Casserole Cornbread

2 c self-rising Cornmeal
1/2 c self-rising Flour
2 Eggs
1 c Buttermilk
1/4 to 1/2 cu Water

Preheat oven to 425F and lightly grease a round shallow ovenproof casserole, or small cast iron skillet.

Mix all ingredients until batter has consistency of cake batter. Pour into casserole and bake for 30 minutes or until puffy and a cake tester inserted into the center comes out clean.

Cut into wedges and serve hot with Herb Butter.

Giving Thanks

My all-time favorite time of year is the Fall. There is no time that feels healthier or more invigorating to me. I love the feel of warm sunny fall days, when the air is crisp and clean. The faint smell of leaves burning somewhere and the sight of squirrels hustling, bustling and burying frantically, reminds me that the cold winter is coming and I should relish these last warm days. Walking through the woods, kicking multitudes of splendid-colored leaves, takes me back to a carefree childhood. It's the best time of year to fall in love, walking hand in hand through the woods.

Having already given up their bounty, the fruit trees are almost bare of leaves. The last few survivors rattle forlornly in the breeze blowing through the orchard. But if you cross the orchard diagonally from the Inn you'll come to a break in the stone wall where there's a gate into the still leafy woods and meadow beyond. In the Fall, when the sun lies slantwise across the sky, the woods seem to glow with a special dappled light especially in late afternoon.

A half mile up the path, if you stop at the lightning blasted old oak tree stump, and look to your left, you can see the ruins of a tiny stone shack. I often wonder about the pioneer who first made the one room shelter. Was he an early homesteader blazing the trail into the unknown countryside. Was he a lonely "mountain-man" or was there a woman, and family, there keeping him company and enduring the hardships. I can imagine Thanksgiving must have been especially meaningful to them: giving thanks for an abundant harvest that would see them through a long winter.

When you return to the Inn, check out the quilt hanging in the diningroom. It's called Autumn Splendor and is a shell pattern design in a riot of green, gold, and rust colors to capture the look of the hills and valley around the Inn. It hangs opposite the window wall, so that it reflects the colors outside, like a mirror. Below the quilt is a long narrow serving table decorated with baskets of orange and yellow gourds, along with juicy red apples, warm brown nuts and a tawny Sherry. Help yourself.

As the sun goes down, friends and family gather and we serve our Thanksgiving feast at an antique rectory table that seats fourteen. Two hundred years later, we give thanks for our abundance, and give thanks to the long gone pioneers who built the little one room stone cabin in the woods.

※ ※ ※

Autumn is the time when I really enjoy making and eating soups. They make light meals yet are warm and hearty fillers after a long brisk walk. Soups usually "age" well and are even better the next day.

Never worry about not having stock or broth to make a soup. Many soups taste just as good made with water. You can make up for the richness that stock adds, by slightly decreasing the amount of water called for, or by adding a splash of wine.

I think country soups are best served in rustic crockery bowls. Always warm the soup bowls before serving so the soup does not cool off too fast, and you can take the time to savor the flavor.

New England Clam Chowder

2 Onions, chopped fine
3 Potatoes, peeled and diced
1/2 c all-purpose Flour
4 c Milk
1/4 c Butter
1 tsp fresh thyme
1/4 tsp Salt
1/4 tsp fresh ground Pepper
2 tins Clams, with juice
6 slices Bacon, cooked crisp and chopped
3 green Onions, chopped
Croutons to garnish

Melt butter in saucepan. Add onions, cook until fragrant but not brown. Add flour, cook over low heat for 5 minutes. Cool slightly. Whisk in milk. Bring to a boil. Add potatoes, bacon, thyme, salt and pepper. Reduce heat, cover and simmer 20 minutes or until potatoes are tender. Add clams and juice and reheat but do not boil. Add seasoning. Garnish with croutons and chopped green onion. Serve with light Reisling white or Muscadet wine.

Cheese and Potato Soup

1 Onion, chopped
2 cloves Garlic, minced
5 Potatoes, peeled and diced
2 c Chicken stock
2 c Milk
1 c grated Cheddar cheese
2 tbsp fresh Parsley, chopped
1/4 tsp Thyme
1/2 tsp fresh ground Pepper
Individual loaves of round country bread

Melt butter in large saucepan. Add onion and garlic, cook without browning. Add potatoes, stock, thyme and pepper. Bring to boil. Reduce heat, cook covered for 20 minutes or until potatoes are tender. Puree half of soup mixture, return to saucepan. Add milk, heat thoroughly. Season to taste. Stir in cheese. Cook on low until cheese melts.

To serve, cut tops of bread loaves. Hollow out, leaving 1 inch thickness of bread to form a "bowl". Brush the inside with olive oil and toast for 10 minutes or until golden and crusty. Ladle hot soup into bread bowls, garnish with parsley, and serve immediately. Serve with robust Cotes du Rhone wine.

Aliske Webb

Harvest Vegetable Soup

2 medium Onions, chopped
3 medium Carrots, chopped
2 stalks Celery, chopped
1 small Zucchini, chopped
2 medium Potatoes, peeled and diced
2 medium Tomatoes, peeled and diced
2 tbsp Butter
2 c Milk
2 c Chicken Stock
3 tbsp fresh Parsley, chopped
1/4 tsp Thyme
1 tsp Salt
1/2 tsp fresh ground Pepper

Melt butter in saucepan. Add onions and garlic. Cook but do not brown. Add carrots, celery, zucchini, potatoes, tomatoes, half the parsley. Bring to boil, cover, reduce heat and simmer 25 minutes or until vegetables are tender. Puree soup in blender. Return to heat. Add milk. Cook thoroughly but do not boil. Season to taste. Serve with a Chablis wine and cornbread. Garnish with remaining parsley.

Grampa's I Hate Peas Soup

When I was a very little girl I hated peas. Who doesn't? My Grampa used to tell me they were good for me and would "put hair on my chest". Somehow I knew I didn't want hair on my chest.... Fortunately I learned to like peas anyway, much to my family's surprise!

1 1/2 c dry yellow split Peas
4 c Chicken stock
2 c cooked Ham, chopped
1 c Carrots, shredded
1 c Onion, chopped
1 c Celery, chopped
2 tbsp Butter

Quilt Inn Country Cookbook

3 c Milk
Salt and Pepper to taste

Wash peas and place in saucepan. Add stock, ham, carrots, onion, celery and butter. Bring to boil. Reduce heat, cover and simmer 3 hours or until peas are tender. Stir in Milk. Add salt and pepper to taste. Reheat to serving temperature. Serve with croutons and parsley garnish and chilled Chablis.

Yankee Doodle Minestrone Soup

(When informed that it was actually a feather that he put in his hat and called in "macaroni", Aliske's response was, "A noodle's a noodle!" Ed.)

4 slices Bacon, cooked crisp and diced
1/2 c Onion, chopped
1 clove Garlic, minced
2 1/2 c condensed Beef broth
1 can Spaghetti sauce
1 can Kidney beans
1 c Water
1 c Carrots, sliced thin
1 c Zucchini, sliced
1/2 tsp Italian seasoning
1/2 c shell Pasta
2 c Milk
2 tbsp Flour
Salt and Pepper to taste

Cook bacon until crisp. Set aside. Cook onion and garlic in bacon drippings until tender. Stir in beef broth, spaghetti sauce, kidney beans, water, carrots, zucchini and seasoning. Bring to boil. Reduce heat, cover and simmer 10 minutes or until vegetables are tender. Add pasta. Cover and simmer 10 minutes or until pasta is tender.

Stir small amount of milk into flour to make a paste, gradually stir in remaining milk. Add to saucepan. Cook over medium heat, stirring constantly until mixture boils and thickens. Add salt and pepper to taste. To serve, sprinkle bacon pieces and garnish with Parmesan cheese. Serve with a red Chianti wine.

Asparagus Soup

1 lb fresh Asparagus *(OK, so make this in the spring, or use frozen!)*
2 c Chicken stock
1 Onion, chopped fine
3 tbsp Flour
3 tbsp Butter
2 c Milk
Salt and fresh ground Pepper to taste

Wash and dry asparagus, remove woody stem. Cut into large pieces and place in saucepan with chicken stock and onion. Bring to a boil, reduce heat and simmer for 15 minutes or until tender. Cool. Place in blender and process until smooth.

Melt butter in saucepan, stir in flour. Gradually add milk and cook until mixture boils slightly and thickens, stirring constantly. Stir in asparagus puree. Season to taste. Reheat to serve. Serve with a Beaujolais wine.

Curried Bisque

1 lb Scallops *(small Bay Scallops will do nicely, or if using large, cut in two)*
1 c Milk
1/2 c Cream
1 can Tomato soup, condensed
2 c Chicken stock
1 tbsp Butter
1/2 tsp Curry powder
2 tsp Onion, chopped fine

Salt
Fresh ground Pepper to taste
Parsley

Wash scallops and pat dry with paper towels. Melt butter in saucepan. Add curry powder and onion. Cook for 5 minutes. Add tomato soup and chicken stock. Bring to a boil. Add scallops. Bring to boil again. Reduce heat to medium, cover and cook for 5 minutes. Stir in milk, cream and seasoning. Reheat but do not boil. Serve with garnish of parsley and a Chardonnay wine.

Presto Pesto Pasta Potage

4 Tomatoes, peeled and chopped
1 Onion, sliced
4 Leeks, sliced thin
1/2 lb green Beans, sliced
4 Zucchini, sliced
1/2 c Cauliflower florets
1 c cooked Navy beans
7 c Chicken stock
1/4 lb Vermicelli pasta
1/2 c Pesto
1 c Parmesan cheese
3 cloves Garlic, minced
1/4 c Parsley
1/4 c Tarragon
1/4 c Oregano
1 tbsp Olive oil
Salt and fresh ground Pepper to taste

Heat oil in soup pot. Add leeks, onion, tomatoes, garlic, herbs, salt and pepper. Cook gently for 15 minutes. Stir in beans, zucchini and cauliflower. Boil chicken stock and pour over vegetables, cook for 5 minutes. Add vermicelli. When pasta is tender, remove from heat. Stir in pesto sauce. Garnish with Parmesan cheese and serve.

Barley and Ham Soup

1/2 c Barley
1 c fresh Mushrooms, chopped
2 tbsp Salt Pork *(or use shortening, but salt pork has more flavor)*
3 tbsp green Onions, chopped
4 c stock from country cured Ham
3 Egg yolks, well-beaten
1 c Cream
2 tbsp Parsley, chopped fine

Saute onions in salt pork until tender. Add barley and stir until barley is coated in fat. Add stock. Bring to boil, reduce heat and simmer 30 minutes or until barley is tender. Add mushrooms. Combine egg yolks with cream and stir into soup to thicken as desired. Serve with garnish of parsley. Serve with Merlot wine.

The World's Best Onion Soup

6 large Onions, peeled and sliced thick
3 whole Garlic heads, peeled
4 1/2 c chicken Stock
2 tsp dried Thyme
2 tsp fresh ground Pepper
1/2 tsp Salt
3 tbsp soft Butter
2 c heavy Cream
Fresh Parsley to garnish

Preheat oven to 350F.

Combine onions and garlic in roasting pan. Add 3 cups stocks and sprinkle with thyme, pepper and salt. Dot with butter. Cover and bake for 1 1/2 hours. Stir pan occasionally while baking.

Remove from pan and process in blender in batches until smooth. Gradually add remaining stock and cream. Return to heat but do not boil. Heat thoroughly and garnish with parsley to serve.

You Say Potato, I Say Tomato Soup

2 c Potatoes, sliced
6 c Water
5 c Tomatoes, sliced
2 c Onions, sliced
1/4 c Butter
1 c Cream
2 tsp Sugar
1/2 tsp Salt
1/4 tsp Paprika

In a small skillet saute onions in butter until tender.

Add potatoes to boiling water. Add onions, simmer for 30 minutes. Add tomatoes, sugar, salt and paprika. Simmer, covered, for 30 minutes. Cool. Process in blender until smooth. Reheat and add cream. Do not boil again. Serve with Chardonnay wine.

"Aunt Ivy's" KORN-TV Chowder

4 tbsp Onion, chopped
1/2 c Celery, chopped
4 tbsp green Pepper, chopped
1 c Potatoes, peeled and diced
2 c Water
1/4 tsp Salt
1/4 tsp Paprika
1 Bay leaf
1 1/2 c Milk
2 c whole kernel Corn
1/2 c Salt pork

Saute onion, celery and green pepper in salt pork until tender. Add potatoes, water, salt, paprika and bay leaf. Bring to boil, reduce heat and simmer 45 minutes or until potatoes are tender. Heat milk and add to soup mixture. Add corn and reheat but do not boil. Serve garnished with parsley. Serve with Sauvignon Blanc wine.

Gumby's Gumbo

1/2 lb Shrimp, shelled and deveined
1/2 lb Crabmeat, flaked
1 lb shelled Oysters
1 1/2 c Tomatoes, chopped
4 c stock (chicken)
1/2 c Onion, chopped
1 tbsp Butter
2 tbsp Flour
2 c Okra, sliced thin
Salt and fresh ground Pepper to taste
Saute onions in butter until tender. Stir in flour until blended smooth. Add tomatoes and stock. Mix in okra stirring until smooth. Add shrimp and crabmeat. Simmer until okra is tender. Add oysters, simmer 5 minutes. Sprinkle with parsley and serve. Serve with a Sauvignon or Merlot wine.

Squishy Squash Soup

1 1/2 lb summer Squash, cut in chunks
1 lb Potatoes, cut in chunks (use Yukon Golds if you can)
4 c Chicken stock or broth
3 green Onions, chopped
3 tbsp Butter
3 tbsp fresh Dill, chopped
Salt and fresh ground Pepper to taste

Place squash and potatoes in large pot. Cover with stock and bring to a boil. Reduce heat, cover and simmer 20 minutes or until tender. Add butter, dill, salt and pepper. Remove from heat. Place mixture in blender and process until smooth. Return to pot and reheat thoroughly. Garnish with green onion before serving. Serve with Sauvignon Blanc wine.

Souper Croutons To Top Them All

6 c Bread, cubed (leave crust on)
3 tbsp Olive oil
3 cloves Garlic, minced
Herbs of choice
Fresh ground Pepper

Cube bread and toss in plastic bag with garlic, herbs and pepper. Saute in olive oil. Remove from heat and dust with parmesan cheese while still hot. Spread in single layer on baking sheet to cool, and crisp. Serve in side dish with soups or salads.

This is a modern "Pineapple" quilt block design. It's a pieced block and is simple to sew because it has only two basic pattern pieces, a square and a triangle, and all straight seams.

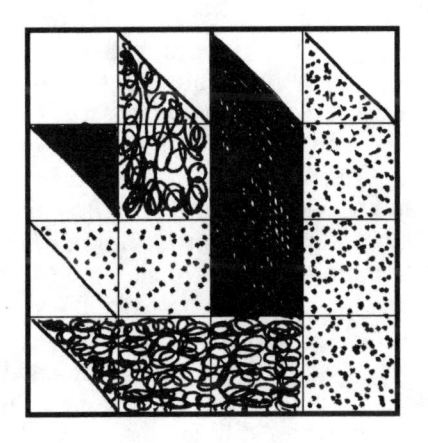

Holiday Memories

  I have to admit to being real goofy about Christmas. Ever since I was a little girl, I've always loved the festivities of preparing for the holiday season. And decorating the Inn is one of the best times of year, in anticipation of guests joining us for the holiday season.

  The main hall is one of the most important rooms in the Inn, and yet we seem to use it more in the wintertime than any other time of year, probably because of the large stone fireplace on the north wall. The previous owners had covered in all the fireplaces in the inn and used them only as decor to hold planters of ferns. We felt that such beautiful old fireplaces should be used and so we opened them all again. In front of the fire sits one of our first, and favorite, antique purchases, a coffee table made from an old farm sleigh. My father recalls using just such a sleigh to haul logs from the woods in the winter to heat the old farmhouse. It still has its original steel runners and the wood struts have been refinished to a mellow dark wheat sheen. A modern top of half-inch thick plate glass has been added, so you can still see the whole frame and the Axminster carpet below.

  On either side of the fireplace are matching hunter green sofas and green-and-gold striped wing back chairs. I have to admit I chose the hunter green decor especially because I love how it looks at Christmas when we add pine boughs, red bows and all the red, green and gold trimmings we've collected over the years.

  In an alcove behind one sofa we put up the tree. For years we've collected tree ornaments around the country. All old-fashioned and nostalgic. We try to find ornaments that are made from wood or cloth, and that enhance a remembrance of Christmas past, Christmas of our childhood.

  The main hall is really important to us for another reason. Michael and I married just before Christmas one year, and move immediately into a huge, empty house. We had nothing in those first days and months except a big house with wood floors and a fireplace and a few boxes of stuff. Our bed was borrowed twin beds that sat in a corner of the livingroom. We went out and bought a barbecue so we could cook our Christmas turkey.

But we had a tree. Our first tree. It had only one set of lights, half a dozen ornaments, and I made popcorn "snow" for the branches. But on Christmas Eve we lit the fire, and put our sleeping bag and blankets on the floor beneath the tree and slept on the floor that night. We kept the fire going all night and the tree lights on. We lay there watching shadows flicker around the bare walls and wondering how we would *ever* fill up the big empty house. (Four years later, the house was so full we started having yard sales to eliminate the obsessive clutter!)

In the morning we drank eggnog for breakfast and opened our presents. Michael gave me a bird feeder and some classical music tapes to replace ones I had lost. I gave him warm gloves and underwear. He's the romantic obviously!

We've slept on the floor in front of a fireplace every Christmas Eve since then. Even the year we were nine and a half months pregnant and had just hosted a Christmas Eve dinner party. The guests went home, the furniture was pushed back and down went the quilts... and three cats... and a dog... and us, Michael, me, and what was to become our son, Geoffrey.

Christmas Eve is also when I decide what to add to my Christmas quilt. I have a quilt that will take me 25 years to complete. It has 25 Christmas wreaths on it and in the center of each wreath I embroider something that represents a significant event for the year. The first was the year we married, so naturally our wedding rings are entwined with the date. I've also added decals and embellishments that are mementos of events, like the teddy bears and baby blocks on the wreath for the year Geoffie was born. Christmas Eve is the time we talk over the past year, and remember.

✻ ✻ ✻

Quilt Inn Country-Style Stuffing

2 c Onions, chopped
2 c Celery, chopped
1 Apple or Pear
1 clove Garlic, minced
3/4 c Butter
4 tsp Sage
1 tsp Marjoram
1 tsp Thyme
1 tsp Savory
1/2 tsp Ginger
14 c Bread crumbs
1/2 c Walnuts
1/2 Currants, Raisins, Dates, Prunes or dried Apricots
1 c fresh Parlsey, chopped
1 c Chicken stock or Cider

Heat butter over medium heat. Add onion, celery, garlic, apple or pear, marjoram, thyme, savory and ginger. Cook for 15 minutes, stirring frequently until tender. Combine bread, nuts, dried fruit, parsley and onion mixture. Season with salt and fresh ground pepper to taste. Toss with chicken stock to slightly moisten if necessary.

Normally, a turkey will hold around 1/2 cup of stuffing per pound of bird. Don't pack it in too tightly or the stuffing will come out dense and soggy.

No matter what you do, you always seem to be left with too much stuffing for the turkey. Place the rest in a lightly greased casserole and cover; place in oven along with turkey for the last 45 minutes cooking time, and you will have extra stuffing for dinner, or for adding to turkey sandwiches the next day.

Aliske Webb

Holiday sprouts

2 lb Brussel sprouts
1 lb fresh Mushrooms, sliced
1/4 c Onion, chopped
1 c Walnuts, chopped coarsely
3 tbsp Butter
1 tsp Nutmeg

Remove outer leaves of sprouts and cut into stem to speed cooking. Steam sprouts for 15 - 20 minutes or until tender.

Saute mushrooms in butter for 5 minutes or until golden. Add walnuts and nutmeg and cook for 1 minute. Toss with sprouts just before serving.

Boxing Day Turkey
(In other words, what to do with left-overs!)

2 1/2 c cooked Turkey, chopped coarsely
3 slices whole wheat Bread
1/4 c Milk
1 Onion, chopped coarsely
3 Eggs, beaten lightly
1 tsp Thyme
3 tbsp fresh Parsley, chopped
2 tbsp Paprika
2 tbsp Butter, melted
1 c Corn oil
2 c Breadcrumbs, seasoned and dried

Soak bread in milk for 10 minutes. Remove and squeeze excess milk out. Shred bread and set aside.

Combine turkey, bread, onion, eggs, thyme and salt and pepper to taste in mixing bowl. Place in blender and process until chopped finely but not pureed. Cover and chill for 1 hour.

Combine breadcrumbs, parsley, paprika and butter.

Shape chilled turkey mixture into large patties. Coat with breadcrumb mixture. Cover and chill again for 1 hour.

Heat corn oil and 1 tablespoon of butter in skillet. Cook turkey patties over medium heat until golden on both sides. Serve with reheated left-over gravy.

Turkey Hash

3 c cooked Turkey, chopped coarsely
3 c Potatoes, cooked and chopped coarsely
1/2 c Onion, chopped
1/2 c sweet (red and green) Pepper
1/2 c Mushrooms
1/4 c fresh Parsley, chopped fine
1/2 c heavy Cream
2 Eggs, beaten lightly
3 cloves Garlic, minced
1 tsp Worcestershire sauce
1 tsp Paprika
1/2 tsp Salt
Fresh ground Pepper to taste
2 tbsp Olive oil

Preheat broiler.

Combine turkey, potato, pepper, mushrooms, onions and parsley in mixing bowl. Combine cream, egg, garlic, Worcestershire, Paprika, salt and pepper in another bowl, mixing well. Stir cream mixture into turkey, coating well and let stand for several minutes.

Heat oil in skillet over medium heat. Add turkey mixture, cover and cook for 5 minutes or until bottom is set. Transfer to broiler and cook another 5 minutes or until top is set and golden brown. Serve with side salad and hot cider.

When I was growing up there was a French Canadian family living across the street from us. They always celebrated Christmas on Christmas Eve by going to midnight mass, then returning home to open their presents and eat their Christmas dinner. Gil always served wonderful Tortiere pies for dinner. We always teased her, calling them "tortured pies". The really great thing, though, was we always visited on Christmas Eve with them -- and opened presents. Then they shared our Christmas traditions the next day -- and opened presents. Their children were younger than we were, so we adults had lots of toys to play with on Christmas day!

Tortiere

2 pastry shells
2 lb ground Beef
1 1/2 lb ground Veal
1 lb ground Pork
3 c Mushrooms, chopped
1 pkg Onion soup mix
1 Celery stalk, chopped fine
4 cloves Garlic, minced
1/2 tsp Oregano
1/2 tsp Tarragon
1 1/2 c dry red Wine
Cornstarch to thicken
Salt and pepper to taste

Preheat oven to 425F

Brown meat in large skillet. Add mushrooms, celery, spices, onion soup mix, and wine. Cook 10 to 15 minutes, stirring occasionally. Make paste of 3 tbsp cornstarch and 1/4 c water. Thicken meat mixture. Cool slightly. Fill pieshell and cover with pastry. Prick top pastry with knife. Bake for 25 to 30 minutes. Top pastry should be golden brown. Serve with crisp dill pickles, mashed potatoes (try Pesto Potatoes, below) and vegetable of choice. Serve with a robust Burgundy wine.

Tortieres can be made up in advance and frozen, either cooked or uncooked. Wrap pies (in metal pie tin) in heavy aluminium foil and freeze. To reheat cooked tortiere, leave in foil but pierce foil with knife to allow steam to escape. Heat frozen pie in 350F oven for 1 hour. Uncover and cook another 5 minutes to re-crisp crust.

Pesto Potatoes Please

2 lb Potatoes, peeled, halved, steamed until cooked

Pesto:
1 c fresh Basil leaves, chopped
4 cloves Garlic, chopped
1/3 c Parmesan cheese, grated
1/4 c Pine nuts, toasted
1/3 c Olive oil
1 tsp fresh ground Pepper
1 tsp Salt

Place all ingredients in blender and puree.

Mash potatoes by hand *(I like the lumpy bits, it seems more home-made that way)* with pesto sauce and serve.

My Mom has been making these delicious cookies since 1950. The original recipe was German or Swiss but has been changed down through the years. Mom uses Buckwheat honey and makes her own orange and lemon peel -- but you don't have to be as obsessive!

Basler Leckerli

1 c ground mixed Peel
1 1/2 c whole unblanched Almonds
3/4 c Honey (try a flavored honey)
1 1/4 c Sugar Zest and juice of
1 Lemon

1 1/2 tbsp Kirsch or Brandy
4 c all purpose Flour
Dash salt
1 tsp Cinnamon
1/4 tsp ground Cloves
1/4 tsp Nutmeg
1 tsp Baking soda

Preheat oven to 325F

Grind almonds and peel. Set aside.

Mix dry ingredients and place in mound on pastry board. Heat honey and sugar to boiling point but do not boil. Add lemon juice and zest. Remove from heat. Add ground almonds, peel, Kirsch and stir until well blended.

Make a small well in center of dry ingredients and pour in honey mixture. Lightly fold all ingredients together making soft crumbles. Do not make into a firm ball. When evenly mixed and still warm, sprinkle crumbles onto ungreased jelly roll pan or shallow baking sheet with rim all the way around. Use rolling pin to flatten mixture in pan. Bake for 15-20 minutes. Cut into diamond or square pieces while still warm. Brush with a thin mixture of 1 cup icing sugar and 3 tablespoons of water. Allow to cool. Remove from pan and store. These keep well for up to three months -- if they last that long.

My Favourite Almond Fruitcake

2 c Raisins
1/2 c Citron peel
1 1/2 c candied red Cherries, halved
3/4 c candied green Cherries, halved
1 c candied Pineapple, in chunks
1/4 c Brandy
1/4 c Amaretto Di Saronna

Place fruit in large bowl. Add brandy and Amaretto, mixing well. Cover and let soak overnight.

Batter:
3 c all-purpose Flour
1/2 c soft Butter
1/2 c Shortening
3/4 c Sugar
4 Eggs
1 tsp Almond extract
1/4 c Brandy
1/4 c Amaretto Di Saronna
1/4 c Milk
1/3 c ground Almonds
3/4 c whole Almonds

Preheat oven to 275F and grease 6 small loaf pans. Line pans with heavy brown paper and grease.

Mix whole almonds into fruit mixture. Dredge fruit in 1/2 cup of flour until all fruit is coated. This prevents fruit from sinking to bottom of cake.

Beat butter and shortening in large mixing bowl until creamy. Gradually beat in sugar, eggs one at a time and flavoring. Add 1 cup flour until just combined. Beat in brandy and Amaretto. Beat in 1 cup flour, then milk. Stir in ground almonds. Fold batter into fruit mixture until fruit is evenly distributed.

Spoon into baking pans. Bake 50 to 60 minutes for small pans of up to 2 1/2 hours for large ones. Test cake for doneness by inserting toothpick into center. It should come out clean if properly cooked. Remove and cool on wire racks before removing from pans.

If storing cake for a month or so before using, brush with additional brandy or Amaretto and wrap in cheesecloth and then foil. Age for at least 2 weeks to allow flavors to mellow.

Michael's Favourite Chocolate Fruitcake

1 1/2 c raisins
3/4 c candied red Cherries
3/4 c candied green Cherries
1/3 c mixed Peel, chopped
3/4 c dark Rum
2 c all-purpose Flour
1/2 tsp Baking powder
1/2 tsp salt
7 oz. Bitter Chocolate
3/4 c Butter, soft
1 1/2 c Sugar
4 Eggs
1/2 c Milk
1 1/2 tsp Vanilla
3/4 c whole blanched Almonds

Preheat oven to 325F and grease 6 small loaf pans.

Combine raisins, cherries and peel in large mixing bowl. Stir in rum. Set aside to marinate.

Combine flour, baking powder and salt. Set aside. Melt chocolate in double boiler over gently boiling water. Beat butter and sugar together in mixing bowl until creamy. Beat in eggs one at a time. Gradually beat in milk and vanilla, followed by melted chocolate.

Drain fruit, add remaining rum to batter. Gradually beat in dry ingredients. Fold in fruit and almonds. Spoon into pans, distributing evenly. Bake 40 to 45 minutes or until cake tester inserted into center comes out clean.

Cool on wire racks before removing from pans. Brush with additional rum. Wrap in cheesecloth and then foil. Age for two weeks to let flavors mature.

There are as many ways to make shortbread as there are cooks it seems. Here are three different shortbread recipes.

Shortbread Number One

2 1/2 c cake and pastry Flour
2/3 c firmly packed dark brown Sugar
1 c salted Butter, soft

Preheat oven to 300F

Sift flour and sugar together. Add butter by rubbing into flour mixture with hand until mixture forms coarse crumbles. Gather into ball. Knead gently to form dough. do not overknead or dough becomes too sticky. Add a little more flour if necessary. Gently roll dough on floured surface to desired thickness.

Cut into shapes. Place on ungreased baking sheet. Prick with fork. Bake 1 hour or until golden brown around edges.

Shortbread Number Two

1 lb Butter, soft
2 c all-purpose Flour
1 c Icing Sugar
1 c Cornstarch
1 tsp Vanilla

Preheat oven to 300F.

Cream butter until fluffy. Sift dry ingredients together. Fold into butter until smooth. Stir in vanilla. Refrigerate dough until easy to handle. Roll dough into 1-inch balls. Place on ungreased baking sheet. Flatten slightly with fork. Bake 20-30 minutes or until edges turn slightly brown.

Shortbread Number Three

3 sticks Butter, softened
1 c confectioners' Sugar
3 c all-purpose Flour
1/4 tsp Salt
1 tsp Vanilla extra
1/3 c Lemon zest, grated

Cream butter and confectioners' sugar in large mixing bowl. Sift flour and salt together and add to butter mixture. Add vanilla and lemon zest. Blend thoroughly. Make ball of dough and chill for several hours.

Preheat oven to 325F. Remove dough from refrigerator and let come to room temperature. Press into large round cake pan. Sprinkle with graulated sugar. Using sharp knife "cut" wedges into batter. Bake for 20 minutes or until shortbread is slightly browned. Cool for 5 minutes. Cut wedges along pre-marked lines and remove from pan. Cool on wire racks.

Extravagant Party Shortbread

Dip half of each shortbread piece in dipping chocolate:
8 oz semisweet chocolate squares
1/4 bar Paraffin wax

Melt wax in top of double boiler. Add chocolate squares. Stir and mix well until chocolate melts. Remove from heat and briefly dip shortbread in sauce. Work quickly. Place on wire rack or wax paper to cool. If chocolate sauce thickens too much, simply reheat.

Green Tomato Mincemeat

12 c green Tomatoes, peeled and chopped
12 c tart Apples, peeled and chopped
2 c Currants
4 c Raisins
3 tbsp Salt
3 tbsp Cloves
3 tbsp Nutmeg
4 tbsp Cinnamon
5 lb brown Sugar
1/2 lb Suet, finely chopped   *(Recipe can be made without suet.)*
2 c Vinegar

Combine all ingredients except suet and cook over medium heat until liquid is reduced. Add suet. Pour into sterilized jars and seal.

Rhubarb Mincemeat

2 c Apples, diced
2 c Rhubarb, diced
Zest of 1 Orange
Juice of 1 Lemon
1 c Raisins
1/2 c Currants
1/4 c Citron peel, chopped
2 1/2 c brown Sugar
1/2 c Water
1/2 tsp Cinnamon
1/2 tsp ground Cloves
1/2 tsp Allspice
1/4 tsp Nutmeg

Combine all ingredients in large pot. Bring to a boil and cook for 30 minutes or until mincemeat is thick and clear. Pour into sterilized jars and seal.

Cheater's Mincemeat

Don't worry, Grama probably would have done this herself if commercial mincemeat was available in her day.

There are any number of reasonably good commercial mincemeat mixes available. But to enhance their flavor and add some easy home-made-ness to them, to every 1 1/2 cups of commercial mincemeat try adding:
10 oz of applesauce or 5 green Apples, chopped
or add:
1/4 c Maple syrup (or brown Sugar)
2 tbsp Butter
2 tbsp Rum (or Sherry)

Candy Cane Shooter

A delicious holiday cocktail to sip slowly as you do your baking or decorating that tastes like a candy cane.

1/4 oz green Creme de Menthe
1/2 oz Peppermint Schnapps
1/4 oz Cherry Brandy

Gently pour liqueurs in order given over the back of a spoon into a clear liqueur glass. Try this with other combinations of liqueurs. The key is to have each layer lighter than the one below so they don't mix. The higher the alcohol content, the lighter it will be.

Hot Rum Punch

4 c light Rum
2 c Cognac
2 c Cointreau
1 c Sugar

1 Lemon, sliced thin
1 Orange, sliced thin
8 c boiling Water

Combine rum, Cognac, Cointreau, sugar, orange and lemon in heat-proof punch bowl. Add boiling water, stir well. Serve hot.

Eggnog with a Bite

2 dozen Eggs, separated
2 c Sugar
2 c Bourbon
2 c Milk
1 qt whipping Cream, whipped
Dash ground Nutmeg

Beat egg yolks in mixing bowl until thick and lemon colored. Gradually add sugar, beating continuously. Stir in milk and bourbon, blending well.

Beat egg whites until stiff. Gently fold whites into milk mixture. Fold in whipped cream. Sprinkle with nutmeg before serving.

Spiced Tea

2 Lemons
1 1/2 tsp whole Cloves
8 two-cup teabags
2 tsp whole Cloves
2 tsp whole Allspice
10 c boiling Water
2 c Sugar
1 1/2 c Orange juice
1/2 c Lemon juice

Cut lemon into thick slices, stud with whole cloves and set aside.

Combine teabags and remaining spices in large pot. Pour in boiling water. Cover and let steep for 15 minutes. Remove teabags and spices. Add orange and lemon juice and sugar, stirring until dissolved. Serve in warmed punch bowl.

Old-Fashioned Wassail Up-dated

2 qt Apple Cider
2 c Ginger ale
1 tbsp liquid Honey
3 whole Cloves
4 Cinnamon sticks
1 Orange, sliced
1 Lemon, sliced

Combine ingredients in large pot and bring to a boil. Reduce heat and simmer for 1 hour. Strain mixture, discarding spices. Serve in warmed punch bowl.

Christmas Punch

2 c fresh Raspberries
1 pt raspberry Sherbet
1 1/2 qt Cranberry juice
1 1/2 qt Ginger ale, chilled

Combine cranberry juice, ginger ale and fresh raspberries in a chilled punch bowl. Drop sherbet by scoops into punch. Serve immediately.

Icy Christmas Coffee

6 oz strong Coffee
2 tsp Sugar
2 tsp Creme de Menthe *(or syrup if you prefer non-alcoholic)*
1/4 tsp Mint extract
1 scoop vanilla Ice Cream
Ice cubes

Combine ice, coffee and sugar in tall glass. Stir to dissolve sugar. Add creme de menthe (or syrup), mint extract and ice cream. Serve with Candy Cane hooked over edge of glass.

Christmas Carollers' Chocolate

For each person to be served:
melt 2 ounces of good quality semisweet chocolate in top of double boiler (or microwave, I suppose) then whisk in 1 cup milk and heat thoroughly

Snowballs in the Mud

Prepare hot chocolate as above, and to each mug of chocolate add 1/4 teaspoon of mint extract (for children) or 1/2 teaspoon Creme de Menthe (for grownups). Float marshmallow "snowballs" on top and serve with Chocolate Mint Stick.

A Note From The Author

People often ask us where The Quilt Inn is located and when they can come visit us. The first answer is: anytime your heart, and imagination, travels through these pages, you have visited us.

The second answer is less poetic, and demands a longer explanation. Michael and I are both goal-setters. We have a ten year goal to buy, build and/or establish a country inn. The inn will be not only an inn in a pleasant country setting, but also a spa and meeting center where guests can attend personal growth seminars, or cooking and quilting classes, or just laze around, of course.

Because I am a passionate quilter, the name The Quilt Inn was decided upon early in our action plan, in order to give us a real visualization of the final goal. We've been developing and testing recipes for our guests-to-be, and, we've been collecting antiques to furnish the inn. Short of finding the actual bricks and mortar, the inn is already as real as it could be. In fact, one year for Christmas Michael presented me with a custom-made old-fashioned wrought iron sign to hang outside "The Quilt Inn" -- an even more "real" visualizing technique. The sign travels with us everywhere around the country on our quest for the ultimate inn.

In the meantime, The Quilt Inn Printworks, Inc. became the name for our publishing company as a vehicle for sharing our ideas and ideals with people like you, dear reader. So, thank you for your interest in The Quilt Inn. And we look forward to meeting you someday in real-time, at "The Quilt Inn".

                                        Aliske Webb
                                        Toronto, 1993

Index

Antipasto, Peach, 8
Apple French Toast, 8
Apple
  Uncle Al Brown's Pie, 77
Apricot Brandy Conserve, 168
Asparagus
  Soup, 183
  Stir Fry, 132
Aunt Ivy's KORN-TV Chowder, 186
Aunt Ivy's Peach Chutney, 166
Aunt Ivy's Three Fruit Cobbler, 74
Backdraft Chili, 110
Baklava, 104
Barley
  Pilaf, 137
  and Ham Soup, 185
Baserli Leckerli, 196
Beans, Baked
Beans, Green
  Provencal, 138
  Waldorf, 139
Beef
  Hungry Hungarian Goulash, 114
  Stew, Doug's, 114
  Stovetop Stew, 113
  Sunshine Stir Fry Salad, 131
  Tortiere, 195
Bread
  Bruschetta, 55
  Casserole Cornbread, 177
  Catcher in the Rye, 175
  Cornbread, 11
  Country Inn Brown Oat, 172
  Croutons, 188
  Egg, 176
  English Ale, 174
  Fresh Herb, 174
  Fresh Herb Soda, 173
  Graham, 176
  Greek Braid, 174
  Irish Soda, 110
  Pudding with Bourbon Sauce, 18
Broccoli and Cauliflower Casserole, 68
Butter
  Butter Tarts, 72
  Sesame Nutty, 122
  Fresh Herb, 122
  Tangy Orange, 122

Cabbage
  Better Red Than Dead, 83
  Bullwinkle and Boris' Borscht, 84
  Cabbage and 'Shrooms, 83
  Cabbagepatch Pork Chops, 81
  Cabbage Casserole, 87
  Cabbage in the Bac Room, 85
  Coleslaw, 88
  Cordon Bleu Cabbage, 87
  Pasta Cabbage Please, 85
  Pilaf, 80
  Red Cabbage and Sausage, 89
  Sauerkraut, Non-Exploding, 90
  Strudel, 86
  Stuffed, 82
Candy Cane Shooter, 203
Casseroles
  Almondine Rice, 67
  Broccoli and Cauliflower, 68
  Cabbage, 87
  Carol's ABC, 66
  Baked Fish (Greek), 101
  Pork and Potato, 69
  Shrimp, 67
  Turkey Tracks, 65
  Waldorf Pasta, 68
Cheese
  Salsa and, 60
Cheesecake
  Amaretto, 152
Chicken
  Bonnie Stern's Chicken with Fondue, 53
  Firefighter Chicken Stew, 111
  Salad, 41
  Southern Chicken Stew, 113
Chili
  Backdraft Chili, 110
  Harvest Vegetables with, 58
  Pasta Peppers Please, 58
  Salsa, see Salsa
Chocolate
  Chocolate Chip Cookies, 72
  Christmas Carollers', 206
  Dipping Sauce, 201
  Heavenly Hot Chocolate, 147
  Snowballs in the Mud, 206
Christmas Toast, 9
Cinnamon Rolls, 12

Coffee
  Belgian, 125
  Brulot, 126
  Icy Christmas, 206
  Viennese, 125
Cookies
  Baserli Leckerli, 196
  Chocolate Chip Cookies, 72
  Gingersnaps, 76
  Greek Spice, 103
  Jailhouse Molasses Bars, 75
  Pumpkin, 76
Cornbread
  Casserole Cornbread, 177
  Spicy, 11
Crab
  Devilish Crab Puffs, 127
  Salad, 44
Creme Brulee, 153
Crepes, 128
Croutons To Top Them All, 188
Crudities, Copernicus, 145
Date, Nut and Oatmeal Loaf, 74
Eggnog, 204
Eggs
  Benedict, 7
  Swiss Quiche, 129
French Toast, 8
Fruit
  Salad, 45
Fruitcake
  My Favorite Almond, 197
  Michael's Favorite Chocolate, 199
Gingersnaps, 76
Greek
  Baklava, 104
  Braid Bread, 174
  Casserole, Baked Fish, 101
  Cookies, Spice, 103
  Keftedakia, 94
  Opa Okra, 96
  Rice Pilaf, 97
  Roast Lamb, 98
  Saganaki, 93
  Salad, 95
  Shrimp, Baked Au Gratin, 102
  Skordalia, 100
  Soup, Hearty Fish, 101
  Tzatziki, 93
  Zorba's Zucchini, 96
Green Beans
  Haricots Verts Provencal, 138
  Waldorf Beans, 139

Gumby's Gumbo, 187
Hungry Hungarian Goulash, 114
Jail House Molasses Bars, 75
Jam
  Apricot Brandy conserve, 168
  Aunt Ivy's Peach Chutney, 166
  Easy Anyberry, 168
  Michael's Fuzzy Navel, 165
  Peach Relish, 167
  Savory Jelly, 169
  Strawberry Daiqairi, 166
  Strawberries in Love, 169
  Sweet Georgia Jam, 167
Lamb
  Greek Roast Lamb, 98
  Gerry's Lamb Soup, 99
  Irish Stew, Sean's, 109
Meatballs, see Greek Keftedakia, 94
Mincemeat
  Cheater's, 203
  Green Tomato, 202
  Rhubarb, 202
Mint Julep, 5
Molasses Bars, 75
Muffins
  Banana Cran, 14
  Cheesecake, 17
  Cheesey Corn, 15
  Extra Bran, 13
  Hallowe'en, 15
  High Fiber, 16
  Zesty Orange, 17
Okra
  Opa Okra, 96
Pancakes, 13
Pasta
  Pasta Cabbage Please, 85
  Pasta Peppers Please, 58
  Tomato Pepper Pasta, 48
  Waldorf Pasta Casserole, 68
Peach
  Antipasto, 160
  Aunt Ivy's Peach Chutney, 166
  Cocktail, 160
  Chutney, 161
  Pie, 163
  Peach Blue Cheese Salad, 160
  Relish, 167
  Salsa, 161
  Stuffed, 163
  Sweet Georgia Jam, 167
  with Pork Tenderloins, 162
Peppers

Pasta Peppers Please, 58
Chili Slaw for the Brave, 63
Tomato Pepper Pasta, 48
Pie
  Uncle Al Brown's Apple, 77
  Key Lime, 73
  Peach, 163
Pilaf
  Barley, 137
  Cabbage, 80
  Rice, 97
Pita
  Pocket Pita Pooches, 39
Pork
  Cabbagepatch, 81
  and Potato Casserole, 69
  Green Chili Stew with Pork, 62
  Tenderloins and Peach, 162
Potato
  Cheese and Potato Soup, 180
  Lo-Cal Potato Salad, 43
  Pesto Potatoes Please, 196
  Presto Pesto Potato Potage, 184
  Practically Perfect Potato Salad, 43
  Tender Peach Tenderloins, 162
Provence
  Haricots Verts, 138
  Herbes de Provence, 134
  Nicoise Ratatouille, 139
  Quiche de Nice, 140
  Shrimp Nicoise, 137
  Salad Nicoise, 135
  Salad Provencal, 136
  South of France Fish Soup, 141
Pumpkin cookies, 76
Punch
  Christmas, 205
  Galileo, 145
  Hot Rum, 203
  Old-Fashioned Wassail, 205
  Spiced Tea, 204
  Summer, 5
Raspberries in Love Sauce, 154
Ratatouille
  Nicoise, 139
  Tomato, 130
Relish
  hot and Sweet Pepper, 62
Rhubarb
  Mincemeat, 202
Ribs
  Beer and Honey, 24
  Creole, 27

Grown Up, 26
Hickory Smoked barbecue, 25
Honey Garlic Baked, 22
Marinade:
  California, 34
  Ginger, 33
  Lemon Baster, 34
  Tex Mex, 34
  Tandoori, 33
Mediterranean Short Ribs, 28
Oriental Baked, 32
Sauces, see Sauce
Shortrib Soup, 35
Southern Style, 30
Stuffed, 29
Sweet and Sour Broiled, 23
Very Merry Baked, 24
Rice
  Pilaf, Greek, 97
  Pudding
    From Scratch, 10
    Left-over, 10
  Salad, 41
Saganaki, 93
Salad
  Angela's Summer Seafood, 38
  Chicken, 41
  Chili Slaw, 63
  Classic Caesar, 39
  Classico Tomato, 49
  Crab, 44
  Crazy Quilt Fruit, 45
  Greek, 95
  Lo-Cal Potato, 43
  Nicoise, 135
  Northern California, 42
  Peach Blue Cheese, 160
  Practically Perfect Potato, 43
  Provencal, 136
  Quilt Inn, 131
  Rice, 41
  Southern California, 42
  Sunshine Stir Fry, 131
  Curried, 40
Salsa
  Cooked, 60
  Fresh, 59
  and Cheese, 60
  Creamy Salsa Dip, 61
  Peach, 161
Salmon Souffle, 133
Sauces
  Barbecue:

    Southern Style, 30
    Racetrack, 30
    Molasses, 31
    To the Manor Born, 31
    Yuppie, 31
  Chocolate Dipping, 201
  Curry, 121
  Egg-Lemon (Greek), 99
  English Custard, 123
  Grand Marnier, 154
  White Garlic, 118
  Red Garlic, 118
  Green Garlic, 119
  Horseradish and Sausage, 120
  Hot Toddy Rum, 123
  Hot Wine, 157
  Mustard, 121
  Peppery Orange, 120
  Pest, 196
  Raspberries in Love, 154
  Skordalia (Greek), 100
  Classic Thick Tomato, 54
  Umbeto's Famous Pasta, 52
  Zucchini Garlic, 119
Sauerkraut, Non-Exploding, 90
Sausage
  Red Cabbage and Sausage, 89
  Hearty Quilt Inn Salad, 131
Shortbread, 200
  Dipped in Chocolate, 201
Shrimp
  Baked Shrimp Au Gratin, 102
  Casserole, 67
  Nicoise, 137
Skordalia (Greek), 100
Spinach
  My Dear Madeira Spinach, 156
Stew
  Beef, Doug's, 112
  Firefighter Chicken, 111
  Irish, 109
  Southern Chicken, 113
  Stovetop, 114
Souffle, Salmon, 133
Soup
  Asparagus, 183
  Aunt Ivy's Chowder, 186
  Barley and Ham, 185
  Bullwinkle and Boris' Borscht, 84
  Cheese and Potato, 180
  Curried Bisque, 183
  Harvest Vegetable, 181
  Hearty Fish (Greek), 101

  Gerry's Lamb, 99
  Grampa's I Hate Peas, 181
  Gumby's Gumbo, 187
  Madeira, 157
  New England Clam, 179
  Potato, Tomato, 186
  Presto Pesto Potato Potage, 184
  South of France Fish, 141
  Shortrib, 35
  Squishy Squash, 187
  Souper Croutons, 188
  Tomato, 47
  World's Best Onion, 185
  Yankee Doodle Minestrone, 182
Sprouts, Holiday, 193
Tamara's Mother's Savory
    Cabbage Strudel, 86
Tomato
  Bonnie Stern's Chicken with
    Tomato Fondue, 53
  Bruschetta, 55
  Classico Tomato, 49
  Cool Tomato Soup, 47
  Fried Red Tomatoes, 48
  Green Tomato Mincemeat, 202
  Oriental Tomato Salad, 50
  Classic Thick Tomato Sauce, 54
  Ratatouille, 130
  Stuffed, 50
  Tomato Pepper Pasta, 48
  Umberto's Famous Pasta Sauce, 52
Tortiere, 195
Turkey
  Boxing Day Turkey, 193
  Hash, 194
  Drunkard's Path, 155
  Pot Pie with Herb Crust, 108
  Quilt Inn Country Stuffing, 192
Tzatziki, 93
Uncle Al Brown's Apple Pie, 77
Zucchini
  Zucchini Garlic Sauce, 119
  Zorba's Zucchini, 96

The Quilt Inn Country Cookbook

If you enjoyed this book...

It makes a wonderful gift
for Mother's Day, Christmas
Valentine's Day, Birthdays...

Use the Order Form below and forward to:
Aliske Webb
24 Farmcrest Drive
Scarborough, Ontario
Canada M1T 1B7

Please send _____ copies of Scrap Quilt Memories
 _____ copies of Twelve Golden Threads
 _____ copies of The Quilt Inn Country Cookbook
to me or someone I love: (We will enclose a gift card from you)

Name: _____

Address: _____

_____ Postal/Zip _____

Method of Payment: ☐ Cheque enclosed

☐ Visa   ☐ American Express

Card # _____ Expiry Date _____

Signature _____

Amount: _____ x $ 9.95 = $ _____
         _____ x $14.95 = $

Postage & Handling $ 3.50
(Ont. residents add 8% PST) $
(Cdn. residents add 7% GST) $ _____

TOTAL $ _____

If you enjoyed this book...

Look for these other books from
Best Selling author Aliske Webb

"Twelve Golden Threads"
$9.95
*Lessons for Successful Living
from Grama's Quilt*

"Scrap Quilt Memories"
$9.95
*An inspiring Heroine's
Journey*

For information
or to order, write to

The Quilt Inn Printworks Inc.
24 Farmcrest Drive
Scarborough, Ontario
Canada M1T 1B7